SEATTLE UNIVERSITY

A

Century of Jesuit

Education

SEATTLE UNIVERSITY

A

Century of Jesuit

Education

BY WALT CROWLEY

PRINCIPAL PHOTOGRAPHY BY
FR. BRAD REYNOLDS, SJ, AND
CHRIS NORDFORS

DESIGNED BY MARIE McCAFFREY
PRODUCED BY CROWLEY ASSOCIATES, INC.

PUBLISHED BY SEATTLE UNIVERSITY
ON THE OCCASION OF ITS CENTENARY
1991

FR. WILLIAM J. SULLIVAN, SJ, PRESIDENT

MEMBERS OF THE BOARD OF REGENTS

(Since its establishment in 1951; in alphabetical order with terms of service)

SEATTLE UNIVERSITY

A Century of Jesuit Education

First Printing: 2,000 Copies Issued on September 27, 1991.

Produced by Crowley Associates, Inc, Seattle, Washington, for the Seattle University
Centennial Committee: Zia Gipson, Coordinator • Margaret Ainsley • Benes Aldana
Len Beil • Ron Bennett • Paul Blake • Catherine Brownell • Mark Burnett • Lorena
Calvillo • Joyce Crosby • Jan Dwyer • Winfield Fountain • Terri Gaffney • Roger Gillis
Clare Grausz • Kathye Grisham • Cathy Haffner • Wanda Haynes • Robert Heeren
Robert Johnson • Mary Malarkey • Terry Marinkovich • Luis Moreno • Peter Nickerson
Carol Penny • Fr. James Royce, SJ • Valerie Ryan • Jeremy Stringer
Fr. John Topel, SJ • Sidneye Trowbridge • Peter Truex • Jennifer Velling
and Delight Willing.

Production of this book was supervised by the Seattle University Centennial Book
Committee: Mary Malarkey, chair • Paul Blake • Fr. Emmett Carroll, SJ • Joyce Crosby
Fr. Louis Gaffney, SJ • Zia Gipson • Beth Grubb • William Guppy • J. Robert Larson
Fr. William LeRoux, SJ • Fr. James Royce, SJ • Fr. William Sullivan, SJ
and Valerie Ryan.

Text set in Century Old Style by Neographics, Seattle. Headings set in Garamond Book
Condensed by Thomas & Kennedy, Seattle. Photographic services by Wagner Photolab,
Seattle. Color separations by Graphic Chromatics, Seattle. Printed by Frayn Printing,
Seattle. Bindery by Lincoln & Allen, Portland, Oregon.

Selected photographs printed with permission of Wallace Ackerman Studios
Genevieve Albers • Paul Dorpat • Gregg Krogstad • Charles McHugh • John and Jeanne
O'Brien • Millie Russell • Sisters of Providence Archives, Seattle • Society of Jesus
Oregon Provincial Archives, Gonzaga University, Spokane, Washington • and
Ann Wyckoff. All other photographs are property of Seattle University.

ISBN 0-9630691-0-1

Inquiries regarding this book should be directed to:
Vice President for University Relations
Seattle University
Broadway and Madison Street
Seattle, Washington 98122-4460
(206) 296-6100

SEATTLE UNIVERSITY
A
Century of Jesuit Education

TABLE OF CONTENTS

Father William J. Sullivan, SJ, became Seattle University's 20th president on May 3, 1976. (Fr. Brad Reynolds, SJ)

Inset: Proud students beam after receiving their diplomas in 1991. (Chris Nordfors)

PRESIDENT'S WELCOME

Founded in 1891 by two Jesuit priests as a school for Catholic boys, Seattle University is now the Northwest's largest independent institution of higher education. This book traces the university's history through its centennial year.

A centennial year represents an axial moment in the history of an institution. It brings with it a powerful invitation to reread our history and to draw meaning from its lessons. At the same time, the centennial moment carries with it a strong incentive to think seriously about the future, to plan, and to dream.

Seattle University's centennial year of 1991 provided both the opportunity and the inspiration for a number of us to reflect upon the various chapters in the history of the institution. For me personally, immersion in the details of the university's history (people, buildings, events) led to a much deeper understanding of our heritage — and deepened my appreciation of the centennial celebration.

Most especially, I came to appreciate the initiative, dedication, and hard work of the men and women who have worked and studied here over the past century, often under conditions considerably more difficult than those we face today. Without their struggles, there would be no Seattle University in the 1990s. Understanding the commitment of these people is both humbling and energizing for those of us working to build on the foundation they laid.

Almost the entire first century of Seattle University has been a time of struggle. The lack of resources at the beginning, the dearth of students, the exodus to Roanoke Street for 13 years, the impact of World War II and the Vietnam War, the rapid turnover of presidents in the late Sixties and early Seventies — all these factors paint a picture of adversity far greater than that experienced by many other American universities.

One clear lesson of our history is this: persistence and dedication in the face of tremendous odds unified and tempered Seattle University. A will to survive, a desire to serve, a sense of mission, and a strong faith carried Seattle University through these troubled times. Institutional character prevailed.

My own enhanced understanding of Seattle University's history has led me to realize how quickly and significantly the institution has changed. The Seattle University of 1941 would be unrecognizable today. There are two major causes for this extensive change: the G.I. Bill and the Second Vatican Council. The G.I. Bill brought to the university a huge influx of students from diverse racial, religious, and socio-economic backgrounds, and led to significant permanent enrollment growth. Vatican II changed the university internally. As the Church's image of itself in relation to other religions and the secular world was reformed, the university's mission, programs, clientele, and faculty all changed in an irreversible way.

A second clear lesson, then, is that a university is necessarily dynamic. Change and growth are integral characteristics of our institution. Seattle University has prospered because it has welcomed change rather than resisted it.

While it is good to invite and accept change and growth, it is equally important that an institution understand and reinforce those characteristics which define it and make it unique. Seattle University has always been true to several defining commitments: to academic excellence in teaching and learning, to education in values, to service, and to the institution's religious character. Though this character has changed since Vatican II, it has remained at the core of our self-image — to a greater degree than at most religiously-sponsored colleges.

This leads us to a third clear lesson of our history: retaining its commitment to its central religious and pedagogical values has strengthened Seattle University. The difference between

Seattle University and other institutions in this regard lies, I believe, in the presence of an active Jesuit community which served to stoke the fires of the religious ethos at Seattle University.

The continued success of our university will depend largely on how well we understand these and other lessons of our first century and apply them to the challenges which will face us in the next 100 years. We must remain true to our heritage, our values, and our institutional character as we formulate the goals, ideals, and dreams which will direct us into our second century.

I hope and dream that someday Seattle University will be, and will be recognized as, the premier independent comprehensive university in the Northwest. Our excellence must be measured in the total educational impact we have on the lives of all of our students. We need to change our students by helping them explore appropriate values and personal ideals. We must help them attain knowledge and master professional and interpersonal skills. We must enable our students to grow as persons in new dimensions.

If we are to achieve true excellence, we must increase the extent and the quality of our service to the urban world which is our home. Seattle University is not, and has never been, an ivory tower. Now, however, in a period of unprecedented urban distress across the nation, we must envisage new ways to interact with our city and to educate our students for successful urban living.

The excellence for which we strive has its roots in the Jesuit and Catholic traditions which have shaped Seattle University since its founding. That is our ongoing commitment to being a center for the formation of men and women in their moral and ethical spheres. In the Jesuit tradition, we must continue to bring values and moral reasoning not only to the humanities but also — and particularly — to science, business, engineering, nursing, teacher preparation, and

Soccer dominates the use of the university's new intramural fields. (Steve Meltzer).

Spring blossoms frame the Administration Building. (Chris Nordfors)

The landscape artistry of Fr. Ray Nichols, SJ, and Fugitaro Kubota survives in this serene retreat below Campion Hall and in other campus plantings (Greg Krogstad). Students grab a bite to eat in Ballarmine Hall's "Marketplace" cafe (Chris Nordfors).

Students confer in the Bannan Center (Chris Nordfors), which is busy with evening classes long after darkness falls (Gregg Krogstad).

The skylights of the Life Sciences "grotto" glow at night, while daylight floods the atrium of the Casey Building. (Gregg Krogstad)

other areas of professional education. One challenge which faces us, if we are to be recognized as the Northwest's singular outstanding independent comprehensive university, is to serve as a model for other universities seeking to educate professionals with a strong moral sense.

Just as we must strive toward recognizable excellence, so too must we work to maintain our Catholic and Jesuit character. The values of Jesuit education have always provided anchor and direction for Seattle University, in no small part because of the significant Jesuit presence among trustees, administrators, and faculty. Every president of the university has been a Jesuit. As the number of Jesuits on campus continues to decline, and as the university looks to a period when lay leadership is a very real possibility,

we must recognize that the anchor and direction historically provided by Jesuits must come from elsewhere. We must rededicate ourselves to the values of Jesuit education — academic excellence, values and moral reasoning, service to the community, holistic growth of students — even in the absence of a Jesuit community. This will be a major challenge for Seattle University in its second century.

The issue of Seattle University's future greatness is, above all, an issue of spirit or ethos. As I have reflected on this axial moment of our centennial, I ask how we can be true to our roots, to our tradition, and to the mission that has grown out of them. It is apparent to me that the lessons of the past play a major role in addressing the challenges of the future. Those people who will shape the institutional ethos in the coming years would do well to start with a careful examination of our university's first century.

This book provides a good starting point. As we began to prepare for our centennial, it quickly became evident that the centennial provided a wonderful opportunity for sharing our history. We realized that, among the tens of thousands of loyal alumni and friends of Seattle University, very few have more than the most general knowledge of the institution's history. Many of the Jesuits have read Father Tim Cronin's history of Seattle University's first 75 years; however, that scholarly dissertation was never disseminated to a wider audience.

The centennial was an ideal occasion to commission a popular history. Accordingly, we asked local journalist Walt Crowley to research and write a history of Seattle University's first hundred years. The result, as you will find, is quite impressive: a history that is accurate, informative, anecdotal, interesting, and eminently readable.

William J. Sullivan, S.J.

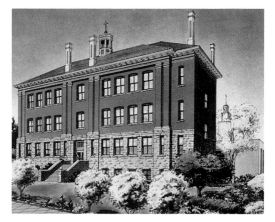

The Casey Building (left) houses Liberal Arts faculty and "Commons" dining hall. Plans call for restoring the Garrand (top) Building to its original 1894 appearance. The Bessie Burton Skilled Nursing Residence is the latest addition to campus.

Overleaf: Seattle University's Jesuit community gathered on the steps of the Lemieux Library in 1986. (Brad Reynolds, SJ)

Inset: St. Ignatius of Loyola secured a Papal charter for the Society of Jesus in 1540. (Oregon Provincial Archives)

THE JESUIT MISSION

M any paths intersect at Broadway and Madison, the home of Seattle University. It is a crossroads for the Catholic Faith, Jesuit tradition, modern learning, and the evolution of Seattle and the entire Pacific Northwest. As these strands have come together, there have been collisions and snarls, but more importantly, a greater merging and synthesis.

The purpose of this book is to retrace the routes that led to Seattle University in its centennial year, but one cannot understand how the university came to the place it occupies today without following the strands of Catholic and Jesuit tradition that define its mission and philosophy.

As a Catholic university, Seattle University is part of a spiritual, intellectual and institutional continuum stretching back two millennia. It embodies and expresses a shared faith, philosophy, history and community. Seattle University is not limited to Catholics — indeed, only half of its enrollment belongs to the Church — but it has a point of view, a purpose and a style which are shaped by its Catholic heritage.

Paramount among these is a special idea of the intellect as a doorway to God. In the Catholic way of knowledge, an understanding of the world is not merely found, it is revealed through a providence which not only gives men and women the ability to think but which acts positively to reward enquiry with comprehension and spiritual discovery.

In this Catholic tradition, investigation and instruction are vital forms of reverence premised on a faith that every individual can find, by the grace of God, his or her own truth. Thus, Seattle University is faithful to its Catholic roots without operating exclusively or even chiefly for Catholics. It is not a religious school offering only catechism or theology. On the contrary, Seattle University is a leading institution in such traditionally secular fields as computer science, psychology, engineering, education, nursing, and business, and it attracts faculty, staff and students representing every religious persuasion.

Within the broad Catholic intellectual tradition, Seattle University follows a special vector founded and extended by the Society of Jesus, an order of Catholic priests established more than 450 years ago by Ignatius of Loyola, a Basque nobleman now revered as a Saint. It is difficult to imagine a less likely candidate for launching one of history's greatest continuing experiments in applied intellect.

Don Inigo Lopez de Loyola y Onaz was born in his family's ancestral Pyrenees castle in 1491 as Muslims and Christians struggled for control of Spain. Ignatius (as he later became known) displayed no early religious enthusiasm and led a fairly typical life as a young courtier and soldier until, at the age of 30, he received a severe leg wound in a battle with the French.

Ignatius retired to Loyola for a long convalescence. He read to pass the time and soon exhausted the supply of novels in the family library. Out of boredom Ignatius turned to religious texts to fill the hours, but recreation became revelation. After reading about the lives of Christ and the Saints, Ignatius resolved to emulate them by making a pilgrimage to the Holy Land upon his recovery.

His first stop was Montserrat, a monastery outside of Barcelona. While meditating in the nearby cave at Manresa, he began formulating his *Spiritual Exercises* for clarifying and strengthening both the soul and the mind. Thus fortified, he crossed Europe and arrived in Jerusalem, but the turmoil there led Church officials to advise him to depart soon after.

Back in Europe, Ignatius encountered and narrowly escaped the Inquisition, whose agents distrusted all religious novelty. He ultimately arrived at the University of Paris where his ideas served as a magnet for a small but ardent band of followers, including some of the finest minds of the period. In 1537, Ignatius and his compan-

St. Robert Bellarmine, SJ, defended Galileo against charges of heresy. (OPA)

St. Edmund Campion, SJ, won Queen Elizabeth's respect before he was betrayed and executed. (OPA)

Matteo Ricci, SJ, brought Christianity and Western science to the Imperial Court of China. (OPA)

St. Francis Xavier, SJ, established pioneering missions in East Asia and Japan. (OPA)

ions decided to travel to Rome and put themselves at the service of the Church.

This was at the height of the Reformation. Martin Luther was still alive and challenging Catholic dogma and practice, and Europe was alternately scourged by plague, rebellion, and ambitious princes. Amid this chaos, Ignatius and his companions entered Rome and offered themselves to Pope Paul III as intellectual "soldiers of God." Impressed by their knowledge and zeal, the Pope commissioned the Society of Jesus on September 27, 1540.

The Pope granted the Society an unprecedented degree of autonomy, which Ignatius implemented through a series of constitutions organizing the Society along hierarchical lines. The highest official of the Society is the Superior General based in Rome, sometimes called the "Black Pope," who commands the superiors of lower echelons: provinces, missions, colleges and individual Jesuit "communities."

The structure is more democratic than it sounds; the Superior General is himself elected for life by a special congregation of Jesuits, and extensive consultation and individual discernment are encouraged in making and carrying out key decisions. Because members routinely rotate through assignments and positions of authority, today's leader can be tomorrow's follower and vice versa.

While other religious orders put a premium on obedience, what makes the Society of Jesus unique is its emphasis on members' intellectual preparation. Ignatius insisted that students be fully grounded in the humanities before undertaking a vocation as a Jesuit. This process of study, teaching and service typically took 16 years in Ignatius' time. It was guided by the precepts of Saint Thomas Aquinas and the Scholastic philosophers of the late Middle Ages who preserved Aristotle, Plato and other classical thinkers against the chaos of Europe and revived and refined their analytical insights and tech-

niques. The essential insights of Scholastic philosophy continue to provide a foundation — not a ceiling — for both Jesuit education and action.

Such philosophical preparation is essential for missionaries destined to work in the real world far from the security of monasteries, often in distant lands and alien cultures. Each member of the Society must carry the tradition of the order within himself and be able to perceive the transcendent human and spiritual dimensions of whatever and whomever he encounters. For all of the elaborate procedures Ignatius crafted in his constitutions, he ultimately entrusted each Jesuit with the responsibility to discern how best to work *ad majorem Dei gloriam* — for the greater glory of God.

Teaching was and remains the foremost Jesuit mission. Even before giving the Society its charter, Pope Paul III had asked two of Ignatius' followers to help resuscitate the moribund University of Rome, and thereby inaugurated the Society's long career in education. When Ignatius died in 1556, some 40 Jesuit colleges were conducting classes for both clergy and laymen across Europe and in India, Africa and the New World. By 1700, the Jesuit educational enterprise numbered almost 900 colleges, schools and seminaries around the globe. In each and every one of these, instruction was guided by the *Ratio Studiorum*, a rigorous but psychologically astute methodology and curriculum first codified in 1599, which emphasized the education of the whole person in the classical languages, literature, philosophy (including the natural laws of science) and theology.

In keeping with Ignatius' fondness for military imagery, he and his followers called themselves the Company of Jesus, but others soon dubbed them Jesuits, a derisive term for people who carried their piety to excess. So the Society's members confounded their mockers by adopting the name for themselves. During the 16th century, Jesuits spread quickly across Europe and to the far corners of the planet, changing history, adding to knowledge, and serving both humanity and their Church.

Peter Canisius became the first Jesuit to direct a university and led the victorious Counter-Reformation in Southern Germany by force of argument, not arms. At the same time, Edmund Campion debated English Protestants and won the esteem of no less than Queen Elizabeth by his eloquence and literary skill before he was falsely accused of treason and executed.

The great Jesuit thinkers Robert Bellarmine and Christopher Clavius risked censure to defend Galileo and his ideas of the solar system. Before 1700, Francesco Lana Terzi theorized lighter-than-air flight more than a century before the first successful balloon ascent, but he feared, prophetically, that aircraft would become tools of war. Maximillian Hell became the first astronomer to observe the transit of Venus across the solar disc while Rudjer Boscovich studied eclipses and offered a dynamic cosmology that anticipated modern atomic theory by almost 200 years.

These and later members of the Society would even leave their mark on the Moon, whose craters bear the names of 35 Jesuit scientists and mathematicians. This great intellectual tradition continues to the modern day, perhaps best exemplified by the paleontologist and humanist Pierre Teilhard de Chardin who, before his death in 1955, strove to unite natural, social and psychological evolution in a transcendent spiritual synthesis.

But Ignatius commanded Jesuits to live in the world of men as well as ideas, and his followers soon radiated outward to reach every land and culture on the planet. Francis Xavier established the first Christian communities in the East Indies and Japan. Matteo Ricci penetrated China to Peking where he won converts by both his faith and science, and Ferdinand Verbiest later trained the young Emperor K'ang Hsi in mathematics.

On the opposite side of the globe, Jose de Acosta documented the cultures of the West Indies, the history of the Aztecs, and even the physiological effects of high altitudes while researching the Inca postal system in the Andes. Peter Claver cared for the African slaves shipped to Colombia and campaigned against this commerce in misery. To the north, Jacques Marquette charted the Mississippi River and opened the West to exploration and European settlement while Jesuit missionaries withstood torture and privation to minister to the native tribes of French and English America.

Perhaps the most renowned Jesuit missions in the New World were the Paraguay Reductions which established a degree of communal democracy unprecedented in Europe or Pre-Columbian America. These settlements thrived for a century and a half before they were crushed in 1767 in the imperial rivalry between Spain and Portugal. Soon after, the Society faced the same fate.

By the beginning of its third century, the Society had earned a reputation for dividing the house. Depending on the critic's point of view, Jesuits were too liberal or too conservative, too rigid or too flexible, too loyal or too independent. These were not idle judgments; many Jesuits paid with their lives for their advocacy of unpopular ideas. (They still do, as witnessed by the 1989 murders of six Jesuit educators and two lay assistants in El Salvador.)

In particular, the Society's extraordinary successes as missionaries in Europe's new dominions and their advocacy of the original inhabitants' interests inspired the enmity of kings and emperors, who banished Jesuits variously from Spain, Germany and Portugal and their colonies. Europe's rulers finally convinced Pope Clement XIV to suppress the order altogether in 1773.

Although their Society was officially defunct and exiled from most of Europe (a few nations such as Czarist Russia offered sanctuary), former Jesuit priests remained active, if discreetly, with such projects as founding Georgetown University in Washington, D.C., in 1789. Slowly, the Jesuits regained the Vatican's confidence, which decided it needed the Society's services again in the turbulence created by democratic revolution and the Napoleonic Wars.

After Pope Pius VII fully reinstated the Society in 1814, Jesuit missionaries and teachers were soon working their way west across the North American continent, carrying the seed of Jesuit education toward the vast, largely unexplored Pacific Northwest. The idea that those pioneers would ultimately plant and nurture in the form of Seattle University can be summed up in the preface to the *Ratio Studiorum* written almost 400 years ago. Although the *Ratio* has since been retired, the injunction still holds true that Jesuits run schools based on the humanities—

Because they supply man with many advantages for practical living; secondly, because they contribute to the right government of public affairs and to the proper making of laws; third, because they give ornament, splendor and perfection to the rational nature of man; and fourth, and what is most important, because they are the bulwark of religion and guide man most surely and easily to the achievement of his last end.

This is the mission of Seattle University.

St. Peter Claver, SJ, ministered to African slaves sent to South America. (OPA)

Overleaf: The site of Seattle University's campus as it appeared in the 1890s from Broadway and James. The trail in the distance is Madison Street today. (U. of W. Historical Photo. Collection)

Inset: Fr. Peter DeSmet, SJ, established the first Jesuit mission in the Northwest in 1841. (OPA)

I

THE ROAD TO SEATTLE

The Jesuits' entry into the Pacific Northwest was precipitated by one of the most remarkable incidents in the Society's history when four Salish braves from the unexplored interior of Montana arrived in St. Louis in the fall of 1831 — begging for "Black Robes" to minister to their people.

The Society's reputation had preceded it into the Northwest wilderness thanks to the exaggerated legends of Jesuit powers spread by the converted Iroquois who migrated with French Canadian fur trappers into the region. But there were no Jesuits to greet the delegation of Flatheads, as Europeans called the Salish, in St. Louis in 1831. It took two more expeditions and the lives of nine men before the Salish summons was finally delivered into Jesuit hands in the person of Father Peter DeSmet, SJ.

Although Belgian by birth, DeSmet was an American citizen and an enthusiastic advocate of the natives, whom he often captivated by playing his clarinet. A robust adventurer accustomed to the rigors of the frontier, DeSmet chomped at the bit to establish a Jesuit mission to serve the Flatheads and other tribes of the Rockies and beyond.

His superiors were not immediately convinced. While Pope Gregory XVI had entrusted the Society of Jesus with responsibility for missions to the native tribes of the United States in 1833, only two dozen Jesuit priests were currently available for the entire region west of the

Ohio. However, the unique situation of "savages so fervent in religion" (DeSmet's phrase) actually trekking out of the wilderness to request Jesuit priests proved irresistible. DeSmet finally won permission to set out on April 30, 1840, for his first rendezvous with the eager Catholics-to-be waiting in the wilds of Montana.

He did not need his clarinet. When DeSmet arrived at the base of the Rockies the following July, he found over 1,600 Flatheads, Nez Perce and other tribesmen massed to greet him. Traveling back to St. Louis, DeSmet knew that final approval of a new Jesuit "Rocky Mountain Mission" was now just a matter of logistics, not politics.

DeSmet returned to Montana the following year, accompanied by five more Black Robes who led the first wagons into the Montana Rockies. After months of hard travel, they came to a halt along the Bitterroot River, south of Hell's Gate near present-day Missoula. There, on September 24, 1841, DeSmet and his companions established

the Northwest's first Jesuit outpost and named it St. Mary's Mission.

By this time, two other pioneering priests, Fathers Francis Norbert Blanchet and Modeste Demers, had also arrived in the Northwest. Invited by the Hudson's Bay Company to tend to its many Catholic trappers, Blanchet and Demers trekked for seven months across Canada and down the Columbia River to reach Fort Vancouver in November 1838. There, under the protective aegis of Company factor John McLoughlin, they set about establishing a diocese for the growing community of settlers centered at the confluence of the Columbia and Willamette Rivers.

Meanwhile, St. Mary's had become one of the Jesuits' most famous settlements since the Paraguay Reductions, thanks in no small part to DeSmet's tireless promotion of it. First he traveled west to Fort Vancouver to consult with Blanchet — such was their mutual respect that on their first meeting each man prostrated himself before the other — and then east, across the United States, the Atlantic, Europe and finally to Rome, raising funds and recruiting priests and nuns to return with him to the Northwest.

At first, St. Mary's flourished and Jesuits fanned out through the interior of Montana, Idaho and Eastern Washington. To the west, Blanchet was named the Archbishop of Oregon City in 1846. His brother, Augustin Magliore Blanchet, traveled from Canada to take his post as Bishop of Walla

St. Mary's Mission near present-day Missoula became world-famous in the 1840s. (OPA)

Fr. Joseph Cataldo, SJ, put more faith in Spokane's future than Seattle's. (OPA)

Fr. DeSmet didn't need his clarinet to captivate "savages so fervent in religion." (OPA)

Walla, while Demers was named Bishop of Vancouver Island to assist in the administration of the vast territory from the Oregon border to lower British Columbia and from the Montana Rockies to the Pacific. The region's scattered residents included perhaps a thousand confirmed Catholics, served by four Oblate Fathers, 13 Diocesan priests, 13 Sisters, and 14 Jesuits.

These last soon fell on bad times. Although spared the mounting wrath of the natives, who massacred Dr. Whitman and his party of Presbyterians in late 1847, the Jesuits suffered chiefly from being over extended. DeSmet had been reassigned to St. Louis, and was succeeded at St. Mary's by Father Joseph Joset, SJ. Joset had too few priests to maintain his far-flung missions, let alone meet the Archbishop's increasingly impatient requests for Jesuit assistance in the white parishes. Joset had to make hard choices; hardest of all, St. Mary's was abandoned on November 9, 1850.

By this time the British had ceded their claims below the 49th parallel to the United States, and the benign government of the Hudson's Bay Company gave way to the more rigid civil administration of the new Oregon Territory. The latter, along with U.S. military authorities, proved less generously disposed towards the cause of the original inhabitants and their Catholic champions.

The California Gold Rush, begun in 1848, added a new complication by diverting newcomers from the less glamorous business of settling the Northwest. Even Jesuits were not immune to the yellow metal's lure. The Jesuit's Rocky Mountain Mission was reorganized into distinct Oregon and California subdistricts, and its new superior, Father Michael Accolti, SJ, made no effort to disguise his greater enthusiasm for his southern outposts, particularly San Francisco, which he predicted would soon become the "leading commercial place… of the entire world."

It was the practice then to place missions under the wing of established Jesuit provinces which could supply manpower, funds and expertise. So, in 1854, the newly renamed "California-Oregon Mission" found itself attached to the Province of Turin, Italy. This should have strengthened Jesuit efforts, but the new mission superior, Father Nicholas Congiato, further isolated the Northwest's three surviving missions by moving his headquarters south to Santa Clara.

Jesuit morale in the Northwest improved in 1862 when Father Joseph Giorda, SJ, took over as superior of what was once again called the "Rocky Mountain Mission." Giorda relocated the mission headquarters to Oregon, reassigned priests from California to help rebuild and extend the Northwest missions, and he reaffirmed the Jesuits' priority for allocating priests and resources to Native Americans over the white settlers now streaming west.

Unfortunately, President U.S. Grant's corrupt "Indian Policy" combined with the sheer mathematics of white immigration to undermine the Jesuit position. The abuse of native rights and treaties and the Federal Government's blatant partiality toward Protestant missionaries over Catholics broke DeSmet's spirit, and he died in 1873.

The tradition established by DeSmet found a new, indomitable champion when Father Joseph Cataldo, SJ, succeeded Giorda as superior in 1877. Photographs of Cataldo show a small man with an almost elfin face, but history reveals a shrewd, determined administrator whose hand was as firm in guiding his Mission as his heart was soft toward the natives among whom he worked from his arrival in the Northwest in 1866.

The foremost object of Cataldo's affection was the village that would become Spokane and the surrounding tribe of the same name, and it was there that he established his headquarters. Cataldo believed in the destiny of Spokane as the center of a future "Inland Empire." He staked his reputation on it, and thereby helped make the dream a reality.

At the same time, he inveighed against "the

universal neglect of the Indian Race in the American Republic, even by the Catholics themselves." Cataldo constantly reminded his priests that whatever their obligations to the burgeoning white population, *Sumus primo pro Indianis* — we are here for the Indians above all.

Not all of Cataldo's priests agreed. One, Father Victor Garrand, SJ, a young Frenchman recently recruited from the missions of North Africa, went so far as to complain to the Superior General in Rome that Cataldo's emphasis on tribal missions was "out of date and no longer means anything."

Garrand overstated his case; Cataldo was trying to maintain a precarious balance between competing, almost irreconcilable demands. By 1887, with barely a hundred Jesuits, he had rebuilt the native missions, expanded white parishes throughout the Northwest, and founded Gonzaga College (then little more than a high school).

Cataldo had more than enough on his hands when the first letters began arriving from Seattle begging the Jesuits to found a school — and perhaps a college.

First Catholic Church in Seattle

1904

Fr. F.X. Prefontaine overcame his bishop's skepticism to build Seattle's first Catholic Church in 1870. (Sisters of Providence Archives, Seattle)

Seattle counts its days beginning November 13, 1851, when Arthur Denny and two dozen settlers assembled on Alki Point. Exposure to winter storms forced the party to resettle the following February on the eastern shore of Elliott Bay, where they dreamed of building New York Alki — "New York by and by" in the Chinook trader jargon. The village ultimately decided to name itself Seattle after the tribal tyee who tolerated its presence.

The settlers did not abandon their urban ambitions, which received a major boost when Henry Yesler arrived in the summer of 1852 and decided to build the region's first steam-powered sawmill at the foot of what became Skid Road (now Yesler Way). The mill was not yet finished when Bishop Demers visited the hamlet in August 1852.

Demers inquired if there were any Catholics among the few score souls huddled on the edge of the Duwamish River's broad mudflats. Arthur Denny replied that there were none (which was not quite true), but invited the Bishop to offer mass anyway. It was the city's first Christian ceremony and the entire population crowded into Yesler's new cook house on August 22 to hear the Bishop sermonize on charity, which, like Catholics, was also in short supply in early Seattle.

Demers did not tarry in the village and he apparently saw little reason for the Church to devote its scant resources to it. But Catholic influence was strong enough among the natives to offend the town's Methodists. The Reverend Dr. David Blaine, Seattle's first resident preacher, complained that many of "the coarse, filthy, debased natives" had "already learned enough religion through the Catholics to make the sign of the cross and say "Ikt papa ikt sockala Tiee," one pope and one God." Among these was Chief Seattle himself, who was reputedly baptized by no less than Archbishop Blanchet.

A Catholic priest did not set foot again on Seattle's muddy streets until August 1858 when Father Louis Rossi visited on his parish rounds, which included the entire Puget Sound basin. Again, he found no white Catholics, but he paid for two lots for a future church just in case things improved.

Finally, in the fall of 1867, Seattle received its first permanent priest, Father Francis Xavier Prefontaine. A French Canadian like the Blanchets, Prefontaine volunteered for the new Nesqually [sic] Diocese in 1863 and quickly made a reputation as an industrious and popular religious leader. When he landed in Seattle, Prefontaine could find only 10 avowed Catholics out of 600 settlers. Undeterred, he rented a cabin and converted two rooms into a rough chapel. There he conducted his first service on November 24, 1867, for a congregation totalling two white women.

Fr. Leopold Van Gorp, SJ, paid Arthur Denny over $18,000 for Seattle University's original campus in 1890. (OPA)

Bp. Aegidius Junger begged Fr. Cataldo for a Jesuit boy's school "and perhaps a college." (OPA)

The "ecstatic" Fr. Augustine Laure, SJ, pictured at the altar of the old North Yakima mission, became the first Jesuit to visit Seattle in 1890.

The following winter, Prefontaine added two lots to Father Rossi's homestead on Washington Street between Third and Fourth Avenues and began clearing the trees for a new church. At that moment, Bishop Blanchet called on an inspection tour, and was unimpressed by what he found. "Seattle as a mission center was a lost cause," the Bishop declared and forbade construction of a church. Such pessimism may seem shortsighted today, but there was little reason at the time to believe destiny would favor Seattle over Fort Steilacoom, Olympia, Tacoma, Port Townsend, or even Father Cataldo's beloved Spokane.

Prefontaine was not the sort to take "no" for an answer, and Blanchet finally surrendered to his pleas and allowed church construction to proceed, provided no debt was incurred. Funded by parish fairs and the collection plate, Prefontaine finished the Church of Our Lady of Good Help in the autumn of 1870.

Events during the following decade did little to contradict Bishop Blanchet's dim view of Seattle as the population slowly climbed to 3,553. Meanwhile, Tacoma, the self-declared "City of Destiny" surged after winning the coveted terminus for the Northern Pacific Railway in 1873.

Still, by 1876, Seattle was large enough in the Bishop's judgment to warrant assignment of a second parish priest. Meanwhile Prefontaine enthusiastically welcomed the first Sisters of Charity of Providence in 1877. He helped them secure the contract for managing the county poor farm and establish a hospital at Fifth and Madison. Similarly, Prefontaine actively recruited the Sisters of the Holy Names, who arrived in 1880 and set up their first school at Second and Seneca.

The next two decades witnessed a stunning reversal of metropolitan fortunes on Puget Sound. Most would-be cities depended on a single industry and soon stagnated for lack of capital or markets. Seattle's founders had made a point of diversifying their economy and encouraging long-term development rather than short-term exploitation, and the town boomed.

Not even the Great Fire of 1889 (which spared Prefontaine's church but little else in the clapboard downtown) slowed Seattle's progress; if anything, it heated up as the town quickly rebuilt with stone and brick. The census the following year tallied 42,837 residents, almost 7,000 more than the "City of Destiny" to the south and rivalling the far older Portland. Seattle was now the largest city in the new State of Washington, and thanks to the influx of thousands of European immigrants, especially the Irish, its Catholic community was also the state's largest.

By 1890, the current Bishop of Nesqually, Aegidius Junger, had to acknowledge Seattle's dominance and Prefontaine's need for help, particularly in the matter of education. A new, larger Holy Names Academy was adequate for children and young women but male Catholics were left largely to the mercies of secular education. This now included the University of Washington, founded almost thirty years earlier in the heart of downtown on land donated by Arthur Denny, something both Prefontaine and Junger regarded less an act of civic selflessness than unfair competition.

So it was that the bishop and Prefontaine began dispatching urgent appeals to Father Cataldo in distant Spokane. Although chronically shorthanded, Cataldo was curious about this rising metropolis on Puget Sound, which he — and every other Jesuit to date — had somehow omitted from his itinerary during the previous half-century of crisscrossing the Northwest.

For the honor of being the first member of the Society of Jesus to set foot in Seattle, Cataldo selected a young Jesuit, Father Augustine Laure, SJ, who was described by one historian as an "ecstatic Frenchman who had given his heart to the Indians." Laure had only just completed his tertianship (the final year of study and meditation before Jesuit vows) at Sacred Heart Mission in Idaho and had been assigned to Yakima when Cataldo dispatched him to assist Prefontaine during the Lenten season of 1890 and also to serve as his eyes and ears on Elliott Bay.

Laure arrived in Seattle in March 1890 and was instantly won over by the city. In his report to Cataldo, Laure rhapsodized, "This city is beautifully situated on hills, formerly covered with trees where men had to let in daylight with axe in hand. On the east is an immense lake of fresh water. To the west is Puget Sound which is connected to the ocean... The climate is so mild the grass is green all the year round." The Chamber of Commerce couldn't have painted a prettier picture.

Laure departed after a stay of barely seven weeks, but not before confidently predicting that Jesuits would quickly return to establish a college in Seattle. This proved optimistic and by July, Bishop Junger complained to Cataldo, "The people there are down on me for they think that it is my fault" that the Jesuits had not delivered the college promised by Laure.

Cataldo finally responded in the late fall by sending Father Leopold Van Gorp, SJ, his trusted procurator and a member of Gonzaga's original faculty, on a new reconnaissance of Seattle for a school site. After scouring the city, Van Gorp decided on nine lots fronted by Madison and Knight (Marion) Street and Broadway and Williamson Street (Tenth Avenue) in Arthur Denny's newly platted Broadway Addition.

A contemporary photograph shows a scrubby ridge as inviting as a Cascade clearcut, and in those days, just about as remote from the city center. The college-to-be all but surrounded the block's solitary structure, a large frame house owned and operated by the Women's Christian Temperance Union. Van Gorp's choice implied enormous faith in Seattle's future expansion toward Lake Washington. And it wasn't cheap: Denny, who had donated the heart of downtown

St. Francis Hall had become an "elephant" on Fr. Prefontaine's hands when the Jesuits took it over in 1891. (OPA)

Overleaf: When it opened in 1894, wooden steps led from Broadway to the Church of the Immaculate Conception, now the Garrand Building.

Inset: This altar once graced the third floor of the Garrand Building.

Seattle to the University of Washington, demanded $18,382 in hard cash for the Jesuit's campus. Van Gorp put $2,000 down on November 6, 1890, and the Rocky Mountain Mission remitted the balance the following February.

Prefontaine was not content to wait for the Jesuits to develop this site and set about building his own school house at the corner of Sixth Avenue and Spring Street (where the Women's University Club now stands). The elegant, two story structure was named St. Francis Hall, and opened classes for some sixty students in February 1991. The ever helpful Sisters of the Holy Names supplied the teachers.

Volunteer labor was not enough to keep the new school's books balanced, and Prefontaine quickly realized he could not afford St. Francis.

Bishop Junger wrote to Cataldo on April 11, 1891, pleading anew for Jesuits. He explained that Prefontaine's St. Francis school had become "an elephant on his hands" and the Bishop prayed that the Jesuits would "take hold of the school for boys in Seattle and also establish a parish there."

Cataldo's personal feelings upon receipt of Junger's latest plea are not known. He could not have entirely welcomed it since he had just acquired all of Alaska as a new administrative ward to be staffed, in addition to Gonzaga and his cherished native missions, by the fewer than 150 Jesuits at his disposal. Nevertheless, Cataldo promised Prefontaine that he would take over St. Francis until a permanent facility could be developed on the Broadway site.

IMMACULATE CONCEPTION

The Jesuit outpost nearest to Seattle was St. Joseph's in Yakima, as far distant as London is from Paris. The leader of the mission's four Jesuits was the same Father Victor Garrand who was so keen on ministering to the whites that he dismissed Father Cataldo's commitment to the native tribes as an anachronism. Although it was a logical choice, there may have been something impish about Cataldo's assignment of Garrand to Seattle, particularly since the latter was happily settled in his self-described "little paradise" at Yakima.

For all of that, Garrand proved a brilliant selection. A veteran of the Syrian missions, the French-born Garrand had volunteered for the Rocky Mountain Mission and arrived in Yakima in 1885. Although often blunt spoken, Garrand impressed acquaintances as having "a frank and generous nature, open and vivacious, his character was lovable and kind." He also had a showman's knack for liturgical pomp and ceremonial circumstance which delighted his parishioners and students.

To assist Garrand, who was still shy of his 44th birthday, Cataldo assigned Father Adrian Sweere, Garrand's senior by seven years and a recent arrival from the Great Plains where he had directed the Osage Mission. One of the few extant photographs of Sweere, a Hollander by birth, captures an avuncular compassion in his large, slightly protuberant eyes, broad mouth and soft

jowls. A colleague remembered him as "a sincere friend who immediately gained your confidence and whom many priests and religious sought for counsel and advice." Thus, the kindly Sweere appears to have been the perfect complement for the avid Garrand.

The pair departed Yakima in August, leaving the "ecstatic" Laure behind to run the mission (he did so with such verve that he literally worked himself to death two years later), although Garrand remained titular superior. They arrived in Seattle in time to open classes at St. Francis on September 1, 1891.

Twelve days later, Bishop Junger officially announced the establishment of the Jesuit school and parish of the Immaculate Conception. On September 23, Garrand signed the lease taking Prefontaine's "elephant" off his hands for five years at an annual rent of $2,150, an estimable sum in those days.

The following Sunday, September 27, 1891, in a makeshift chapel upstairs in St. Francis Hall,

now named Immaculate Conception Church, Father Garrand offered mass — some 50 years after Father Peter DeSmet had established the Rocky Mountain Mission and 351 years to the day after Pope Paul III had commissioned the Society of Jesus. This date marks the official commencement of the Jesuit educational mission that would lead to Seattle University.

The Jesuit school proved a powerful magnet. "Our school opened with 90 children," Garrand reported. "At the end of the week there were 20 more and the numbers are increasing continually." But Seattle did not as yet have its Jesuit boys' school, let alone a college. Immaculate Conception was a parish school, admitting girls and boys both, and its faculty still numbered more Sisters of the Holy Names than Jesuits. The care and feeding of Prefontaine's elephant quickly drove the new parish into debt, and Garrand had to report to Bishop Junger that he could not even pay the Sisters their token stipend.

Garrand did not carry good news when he traveled to Spokane to attend a conference of mission superiors in the summer of 1892. Cataldo was not discouraged and urged Garrand to press ahead with construction of a permanent school large enough to accommodate two hundred students on the Broadway campus.

This had to wait for the opening of the first full school year at Immaculate Conception. The fall session attracted 191 boys and girls who were greeted by a faculty of, in addition to Gar-

Fr. Victor Garrand, SJ, and Fr. Adrian Sweere, SJ, formally launched Jesuit education in Seattle on September 27, 1891.

rand and Sweere, Holy Names Sisters Claudia, Michael, and John Chrysostom. Another Frenchman, Father Paul Gard, took charge of the older boys and the first steps toward a college preparatory program. Gard was so impressed with the Jesuits that he dreamed of joining them and later, as pastor at Marysville, petitioned for a Jesuit college in his parish. Neither wish was granted but he remained a life-long friend of the Society.

A parish fair was conducted on October 10, 1892, and netted $1,800, only a fraction of what was needed to finance a new school but an impressive showing by a poor parish of mostly German and Irish immigrants. It was enough for Garrand to begin sketching plans for a new building. In March of 1893, Garrand held a "public novena in honor of Saint Joseph to obtain by his intercession the assistance to lead to completion of the building of the church and college." During the succeeding weeks, the Broadway site was cleared and graded and the foundation poured. On Sunday, April 16, Bishop Junger presided over the laying of the cornerstone as parishioners and laborers cheered. A few months later, on June 30, Immaculate Conception School was officially incorporated.

Unfortunately, at virtually the same moment, the revelation that the Federal gold reserves had been drawn down to less than $50 million triggered the collapse of the national economy. The ensuing Panic of 1893 wiped out personal fortunes and banks across the nation and plunged Seattle into a depression from which it would not recover until the Klondike Gold Rush five years hence. This would not be the last time that college plans and the state of the economy proved perfectly mistimed.

Work halted at Broadway, and the open basement and piled stones languished as a monument to the delayed, if not dashed, dream of the college. Garrand and Sweere persevered, organizing "entertainments" and a parish fair. The Parish Announcement Book entry for Oc-

At the turn of the century, Seattle College consisted of the former home of the Women's Christian Temperance Union and the Garrand Building.

tober 15, 1893, records this appeal:

> *Despite the hard times this fair can be a success if everyone contributes his help according to his means... Several members are seriously and devotedly at work, but it is sickening to hear some predicting that it will be a failure. It will indeed be a shameful failure for such ones who will have abstained from work and duty; but it will be a success for all who will have helped at it, because it is a work intended for the church of God.*

The fair ultimately realized $848.25, less than half of the previous year's revenue but impressive given the circumstances. Another school year was already underway at St. Francis. Gard had gone on to other duties, and was replaced by Father James Reade, SJ, who made an instant hit as a producer of school plays.

Garrand managed to find $4,000 that December to buy the WCTU building from his teetotaling neighbors but he could not find a local lender to finance completion of the college building. Unknown to him, a wealthy landowner, Malcolm McDougal, had previously offered Cataldo $20,000 and fifty acres for a Seattle college in memory of his son who had died in an accident at Gonzaga two years earlier. Why Cataldo declined the gift and apparently never apprised Garrand of it is not recorded.

Father Sweere must have maintained some connections in his native Holland because the Amsterdam banking house of the Wiegman Brothers stepped forward and offered whatever Garrand needed at 5 percent per annum. Prudently, the bank also required signatures from the superior of the Turin Province which still governed the Rocky Mountain Mission, the Superior General of the Society, and even the Papal Legate for the United States, since the entire nation was still a "mission" under the authority of Rome's Congregation for the Propagation of the Faith.

The loan was secured in July 1894 and a draft for $16,000 was dispatched from Amsterdam. Garrand already had a crew working on the site when the money arrived. The construction workers were recruited chiefly from the parish and Garrand later recalled, "The Irish wanted to prove to me that their devotion was superior to that of the Germans, and the Germans wanted to do better than the Irish." Without benefit of architect or contractor, Garrand's gang labored "with an energy and spirit that surprised the whole town."

Fr. Garrand's magnificent chapel was unexcelled by any other Seattle church.

They were still working when the new school year commenced. Younger children came to the Immaculate Conception School at St. Francis as before, but older boys were now sent to the WCTU house. By this separation, Garrand further nurtured his *collegium inchoatum*, the seed of the university to come.

As the physical scene of the college was changing, so too was the cast of characters. Sweere had returned that summer to Yakima, and the vacuum was filled by two new Jesuits, Father Stanislaus Polermo, SJ, and, briefly, Father Joseph Guidi, SJ. Reade had been called back east to the Missouri Province and a pair of young scholastics (Jesuits in training), Conrad Brusten and Patrick Mahon, arrived to fill the gap. The faculty was a veritable European Community with a Frenchman, two Italians, a German and an Irishman who, Garrand reported, lived and worked together in "perfect harmony and peace."

The guard in Spokane also changed. Cataldo had returned as an ordinary Black Robe to his beloved Indian missions in March 1893, and Van Gorp was now superior of the Rocky Mountain Mission and simultaneously president of Gonzaga College. Such abrupt reassignments were typical not just because of the need to juggle too few men among too many tasks; the Society routinely shuffled its members' postings to avoid the development of what Ignatius had called "inordinate attachment" to their localities and activities.

Back in Seattle, the excitement mounted as Garrand's new building neared completion. The parish, students, their parents and a curious public finally entered the new structure on December 8, 1894, the feast day of the Immaculate Conception, whose name the building bore. They were not disappointed.

Although he was an amateur when it came to architecture, Garrand had designed a building

whose elemental proportions and sturdy pilasters projected the same Romanesque dignity found in the early churches and monasteries of his native France. He cleverly exploited the slope falling away from Broadway and a combination of stone and brick to communicate that this was really two buildings in one.

Granite blocks enclosed the lower two stories. The ground floor, more a daylight basement, housed the offices and living quarters of the small Jesuit community. The second story contained the classrooms of the Immaculate Conception School and was served by doorways and stairs on the north and south faces. The two bricked stories above contained Immaculate Conception Church, which was connected to Broadway via a wide, wooden stairway ascending to a classical narthex over a trio of arched portals. These were but an overture for the operatic grandeur of the chapel beyond, whose sumptuous ornamentation and mob of statuary would have made many a cathedral seem austere by comparison. Topping it all was a gently peaked roof and an octagonal belfry for the bell which would now order parish life and meter the education of hundreds of boys and young men.

Garrand's love of ceremony had obviously found a new expression in architecture, and he created something the likes of which Seattle had never seen before. The Jesuits gave Father Prefontaine his "elephant" back. St. Francis Hall housed a succession of Catholic organizations as tenants. Prefontaine and his niece even briefly occupied St. Francis before the building was sold and demolished early in the following century.

In 1894, Immaculate Conception Parish embraced some two hundred families, three-fourths of whom were Irish, and they supplied most of Garrand's students. A new electric street car on Broadway and a cable car on Madison made the college convenient for most of the city's Catholics, who numbered in the range of five thousand souls. Garrand moved the parish school's younger boys and girls into the WCTU house, and assigned the older boys to the new building. There they undertook preparatory studies in English, history, mathematics, geography and Christian doctrine. The oldest students were also introduced to the rudiments of Latin and Greek.

Life at Immaculate Conception followed an orderly routine until May 1895 when a typhoid epidemic forced health authorities to close all of Seattle's schools. The danger subsided enough to permit a ceremony on June 8 to conclude the school year at Immaculate Conception, but the disease struck one last victim, Father Garrand. He was forced to spend the summer in his bed, watching the bills mount and trying to marshal what funds he could for both the parish and its poorest members. Garrand's announcements for the period variously implore parishioners to

Sisters of the Holy Names volunteered to teach younger parish children.

Overleaf: Members of the 1902 "Humanities" class, equivalent to college freshmen, pause during a lesson on the geometry of parabolas. The banner bears the Loyola family crest.

Inset: Students pose in front of the north face of the Garrand Building.

subscribe a dime a month to help the destitute, "a sum that almost anyone can contribute," and chide, "Let the ladies of this congregation be a little more in earnest for the sale of the tickets" for the next school fund raiser.

It was not enough, and the growing financial crisis at last demanded Father Van Gorp's personal presence in Seattle. After consulting with Garrand, recovering but still weak, Van Gorp solicited the aid of the Sisters of the Holy Names, who graciously took over the expense of schooling the parish's younger children. This helped in the short term but Van Gorp recognized that the school's survival required more energy than its current rector could now supply. In January 1896, he ordered Garrand to St. Mary's in Pendleton in the hope that the dry warmth of Eastern

Oregon would speed his recuperation.

It did, but Garrand was never to return to Seattle or lay eyes again on the church and school he had built literally with his own hands. Garrand departed the United States in 1899 for his homeland and ultimately returned to North Africa. Before leaving Pendleton, he announced, "I propose to purchase a flag in New York and to go to Egypt with that flag as my emblem of my citizenship. I like this country best of any in which I have been, excepting that [here] the Catholics are rather negligent in going to church."

Once in Africa, Garrand was assigned to serve English-speaking congregations. One of his brothers was working in the region and another had already died there. Garrand toiled dutifully until his own death on March 6, 1925. He is buried in Constantine, Algeria, his final mission.

III

A COLLEGE AT LAST

To take over Garrand's post in Seattle, Van Gorp summoned one of his best mission administrators, Father Alexander Diomedi, SJ, from Missoula. Although it was only an interim assignment, the choice signalled Seattle's rising priority. Diomedi's *Sketches of Modern Indian Life* was already a minor classic in the cultural anthropology of the passing frontier, and one co-worker described him as an energetic intellectual "who would rather argue philosophy and theology than take snuff, though he liked to take his snuff very well." Diomedi remained school master until June 18, 1897, when Father Sweere returned to Seattle, and in a straight swap, Diomedi departed to take over Sweere's duties in Yakima.

On July 17, the steamer Portland pulled into Elliott Bay with a "ton of gold" scooped from the Klondike. The news electrified the nation and Seattle's docks and streets soon overflowed with prospectors on their way to make their fortunes in Alaska. Few of them succeeded, of course, but the gold rush enriched many Seattle merchants and lifted the entire city out of the depression that had lingered since 1893. Immaculate Conception School enjoyed a small share of this renewed prosperity as enrollment in the preparatory program for boys jumped from 42 in 1897 to 73 the following year.

Encouraged, Sweere decided to take the next step in the school's evolution and drew up a charter for "Seattle College where a thorough classical and commercial education will be given." There is no record of any debate or hesitation over the name chosen for the new college. Its founders could have honored a saint or a Jesuit hero, but they chose instead the name of their city, which, it should be remembered, in turn memorialized a great native tyee and a devout Catholic converted in the tradition of DeSmet and Blanchet. *Seattle College* was, in short, a name both obvious and profound.

The State of Washington gave its official blessing to the incorporation of the new college on October 21, 1898. Thus, Adrian Sweere became the first formal president (the ecclesiastical title was Rector) of the college whose seed he helped Garrand plant seven years earlier. He was simultaneously the religious superior of the Jesuit community at the college and pastor of Immaculate Conception Church.

Sweere was joined on the founding Board of Trustees by Fathers Robert Smith and Thomas Neate, SJ (the board was later expanded to five Jesuits; lay members did not join until 1971). For all their theoretical authority as corporate directors, these first trustees were subordinate to Sweere as rector and religious superior. He, in turn, remained under the command of the Rocky Mountain Mission and, ultimately, the superior general in Rome. In addition to the president and trustees, the faculty included Father Albert Trivelli, SJ, and Mr. Joseph O'Hara, a scholastic (a status recognized with the honorific title of "Mister"). By 1899, enrollment had increased to 137 boys who advanced through four levels: first, second, and third "academics" and a fourth "preparatory" year to achieve the equivalent of a public high school diploma.

Of course, there were differences between a public and Jesuit education. The school day at Seattle College began with mass at 8:30 am, and a student was expected to master Latin and Greek as well as the basics, not to mention the fourth "R," religion. The curriculum was still guided by the *Ratio Studiorum*, a Jesuit plan first devised in 1599 for a comprehensive education in humane letters, philosophy, and theology. This curriculum evolved with knowledge and social need, but Jesuit education remained distinct in its emphasis on the liberal arts and especially philosophy.

Seattle College students also had time for a little fun in those last days of the 19th Century. When not developing his mind, the student could develop his body in a tiny gym in the college

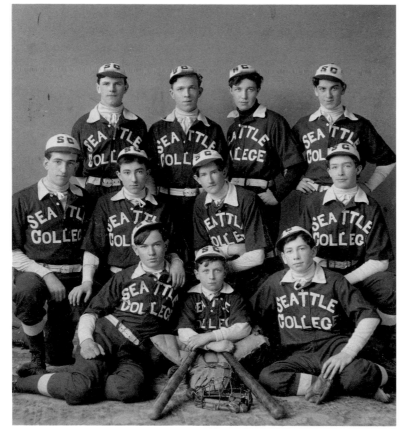

Valiant members of the 1909 baseball team dodged stumps, cliffs and an outhouse on the college's first baseball diamond, which was truly "in the rough."

basement or in the city's first handball courts, located in a shed erected between the college and Broadway. Or he could don the college's first official baseball uniform, which was navy blue with "bright red stockings that almost called out the fire department on sight," according to a memoir written in 1925 by a former student, A.E. Prickett.

Seattle College ballplayers risked life and limb on an ungraded diamond north of the Garrand building. Runners and fielders had to dodge pine stumps, embankments and an outhouse, and Prickett recalled that even victory was perilous:

> *The big event of '99 was the annual baseball game between the "lowly" Juniors and "high brow" Seniors. To insure a neutral playing field an adjoining lot was chosen as the battle ground and for the first time in history the Juniors annexed the scalp of the Seniors in a torrid game with the score 14 to 13. Unlike present day [1925] conditions, though the victors, Juniors were forced to seek safety in hurried flight.*

Enrollment at Seattle College then cost a modest $15 per year, a tuition that did not begin to cover the cost of school operations but which gave the poorest families the option of sending their sons to a Jesuit school. While tuition rose steadily over the coming years, it never caught up with costs, and the resulting shortfall bedeviled most of Sweere's successors.

In the fall of 1900, Sweere introduced a "College Department," consisting of a single "Humanities" or freshman class. The first catalogue, published in 1901, promised the student "the cultivation of his literary taste and powers by reading and imitating the best models of ancient and modern literature." It also set high standards:

> *As educators [Jesuits] aim to secure the gradual and just development of mind and heart together.... It is their aim to form men of deep*

thought, solid principles, virtuous habits, and sound religious convictions, without which they deem education little better than worthless. The formation of Christian character in the classroom is their life's aim.

In 1901, Sweere created the college's first vice presidency for administration, to which Father Edward Brown, SJ, was assigned. The faculty increased to eight Jesuits, while the Sisters of the Holy Names departed. They transferred their younger charges a block north on Broadway to the newly completed St. Rose Academy (this building later became the Marne Hotel, and was leased as a dormitory by the college). The old Temperance Union house was converted into a recreation hall and classrooms for college-level enrollment, although this consisted of only two students in 1903. Preparatory classes, on the other hand, grew large enough to warrant their own yearbook.

Sweere did not have the leisure to focus on developing his struggling college department: instead, he had to build a new church. The new Bishop, Edmund O'Dea, who had succeeded Junger in 1896, announced his intention to move the headquarters of the Nesqually Diocese from Vancouver to Seattle. Because he planned to build his cathedral only a few blocks from the college, Bishop O'Dea asked Sweere to move Immaculate Conception Church to the east, outside of the new cathedral parish.

Sweere selected a site on the crest of 18th Avenue at East Marion and borrowed $65,000 for a magnificent new Church of the Immaculate Conception. The building could seat 950 in Seattle's largest auditorium, religious or secular, at the time. It was a prodigious undertaking for a poor parish, and Immaculate Conception Church's twin spires remain a prominent landmark on the city skyline. Bishop O'Dea dedicated Sweere's church on December 8, 1904, and he must have felt challenged by the modest Dutch Jesuit's achievement as he drew up plans for his own cathedral on Ninth Avenue.

Father Edward Brown was named the college's first vice president in 1901.

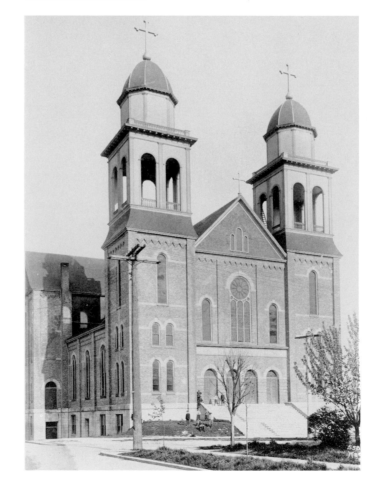

The new Church of the Immaculate Conception opened in 1904. It and Seattle College's first charter are the legacy of Fr. Sweere's term as the school's third rector and first true "president."

Fr. Alexander Diomedi, SJ, succeeded Fr. Garrand as pastor and rector at Immaculate Conception in 1896.

Fire consumed Garrand's altar and gutted its upper floors and roof on May 1, 1907. (Seattle Post-Intelligencer)

Construction of the church, and, thereby, liberation of the college to concentrate on education were Father Sweere's farewell gifts to the parish and school which he had helped to found. In the summer of 1905, he was reassigned to Yakima and ultimately found his way to the missions of Alaska. In 1913, his health failed in Ketchikan and he died while returning to Spokane, where his remains now rest at Mount St. Michael's Seminary.

Sweere was succeeded by Father Francis Dillon, SJ, who became Seattle College's first American-born president. Although not yet 40 years old, Dillon had earned high marks as vice president and then acting president at Gonzaga, and he was reputed to be a trouble shooter for mission superior Father George de la Motte, who had succeeded Van Gorp in 1900. He would have plenty of trouble to shoot, beginning with the debt for Immaculate Conception's new church and revitalization of the school's college program.

Dillon expanded the faculty to 12 Jesuits, and introduced the college's first elective, "commercial studies," including bookkeeping and typewriting, in 1906. An octet was also founded that year and quickly expanded into a 20-member orchestra. The preparatory program attracted 140 boys and 12 young men signed up for college studies, a far cry from the student body of 340 Dillon had left behind in Spokane, but progress nonetheless.

Everything was nearly lost on May 1, 1907, when a fire broke out in the college building's vacant chapel. Students and teachers evacuated the building and did what they could to assist fire fighters. The flames were not extinguished before they had consumed Garrand's glorious altar and gutted the top two stories and roof.

Classes resumed a week later in the WCTU house, now dubbed the Administration Building, and at Immaculate Conception Church while Dillon and his trustees debated the college's future. Permanently transplanting the school

next door to Immaculate Conception Church was seriously debated, but Dillon decided to return to Garrand's original structure despite the estimated $10,000 cost for repairs. The winning argument for staying at Broadway probably paralleled the sentiments expressed the day of the fire by the college's vice president, Father George Weibel, SJ. He told *The Seattle Times*, "This building was erected during one of the greatest financial panics in our history. It represents the devotion and self-denial of our people and it seems tragic that such a monument to Christian love should be destroyed." The lower floors were rebuilt, but college funds did not permit reconstruction of Garrand's chapel, peaked roof and belfry.

Despite the setback of the fire, Seattle's Catholic community was entering a "golden age." The city's population more than doubled during the century's first decade and topped two hundred thousand by 1910. Thanks to immigration and conversion, at least 10 percent of Seattleites were Catholics gathered in 14 parishes. Bishop O'Dea completed his cathedral in 1907 as the center of the new Seattle Diocese and named the edifice St. James, carrying forward the name of Blanchet's original "pro-cathedral" at Fort Vancouver. Bishop O'Dea honored another pioneer in 1907 by securing for Father Prefontaine (who had retired in 1903) the title of monsignor, a final tribute which Seattle's first priest enjoyed only briefly before his death in 1908. That same year, the United States ceased to be a mission territory in the eyes of the Vatican, and the grand new Holy Names Academy opened. The newly arrived Religious of the Society of the Sacred Heart began work on their Forest Ridge complex. The Sisters of Providence began drawing up plans for their giant new medical complex on 17th Avenue, which opened in 1910.

The Society of Jesus was busy, too. The Rocky Mountain and California Missions were consolidated in 1907 under the leadership of

Father de la Motte and attained the status of a province two years later. Also in 1907, St. Joseph's Church opened at 18th Avenue East and East Aloha Street as the home for Seattle's second Jesuit parish, under the pastorate of Father Diomedi. The Jesuits took over their third Seattle parish, Our Lady of Mount Virgin, in 1911 to serve the city's growing Italian "colony."

Amid all this activity and progress, Seattle College had its own cause for excitement. By 1909, enrollment exceeded 200, and 16 men were hard at study in the college department. For the first time, the trustees could anticipate awarding baccalaureate degrees. Fortunately, they took this opportunity to review their incorporation papers and discovered that Seattle College had neglected to include the granting of degrees as one of its corporate purposes.

Amending the bylaws fell to a new president, Father Hugh Gallagher, SJ, who was transferred north from his post as treasurer of Santa Clara College while Dillon was sent south to take over Portland's St. Ignatius parish. Gallagher was the first president to recruit laymen in planning fund raising for the college, and although the initial campaign for a new gymnasium was abandoned, it established a useful precedent for subsequent lay participation in the college's development.

Grander plans could wait while the happy task of organizing Seattle College's first commencement took priority. It was held in Immaculate Conception's social hall on the evening of Wednesday, June 23, 1909. Students performed a melodrama and musical selections for the audience of parents, faculty and dignitaries, and awards were given to preparatory and college students for achievements in various studies.

At last, the names of three seniors were called to receive Seattle College's first baccalaureate degrees from the hand of Bishop O'Dea. They were John Concannon, a future Jesuit who returned to his alma mater as Dean of Men;

The 1911 regrade of the campus transplanted the WCTU house a block east and created a decent baseball field.

A growing enrollment inspired this 1908 plan to expand the Garrand Building.

This 1914 scheme relocated the college next to the original St. Joseph's Church.

Students lampoon college life by performing "The Freshman" in 1915.

From the top: Jesuit fear of "inordinate attachment" prompted a rapid turnover of Seattle College presidents: In 1910, Father Charles Carroll, SJ, succeeded Fr. Hugh Gallagher, SJ, who in 1907 had succeeded Fr. Francis Dillon, SJ, who in 1905 had succeeded Fr. Sweere.

John Ford, who later made his mark as a successful businessman; and Theodore M. Ryan, destined to become the first Seattle native to be ordained a priest. Ryan rose in the Church to become a monsignor in the Seattle Diocese and pastor of Immaculate Conception when the Jesuits ceded the parish to the Diocese in 1929.

The ceremonies ended with the three graduates forming into a triumphant march. It was a very short procession, but more would follow, for Seattle College was finally, if barely, a college in more than name.

The 1909/10 school year began with another change in the presidency as Father Gallagher was suddenly reassigned to Yakima. The Ignatian injunction against "inordinate attachment" was becoming an obstacle to ordinary administration. At least the new president, Father Charles Carroll, SJ, knew something about the college, having just completed his final year as a scholastic teaching there.

Newly ordained and only 33 years old, Car-

roll attacked his duties with youthful enthusiasm and bold plans. He was very much in tune with the spirit of the entire city. The years before the Great War bubbled over with what H.G. Wells called America's unique "fatalistic optimism," and Seattle celebrated its own manifest destiny in 1909 with the vast Alaska-Yukon-Pacific Exposition which gave the University of Washington its present campus.

Social reformers charged back and forth across the political landscape, challenging "demon rum," poverty and other evils while promoting radical innovations such as women's suffrage and labor's right to organize. And City Engineer R.H. Thomson set about reshaping the physical landscape, sluicing away hills and humbling steep ridges from one end of Seattle to the other. Not to be outdone, Father Carroll contracted to regrade the precipitous drop east of Broadway, which steam shovels and graders attacked and tamed in 1911. During the operation, the college jacked the WCTU house down the slope and replanted it on 10th at Madison.

One benefit of all this earthmoving was a decent playing field, of which Father Francis Burke, SJ, who introduced baseball at Gonzaga, soon became undisputed king. In *Reminiscing*, a collection of memoirs of the period, Archie Richardson (class of 1927) recalls that Burke's fly balls routinely sailed over Broadway and Madison, variously smashing windows in the Broadway Building on the northeast corner or splitting the awning of Gus Blana's grocery on the northwest corner. When Richardson went to retrieve one ball, the grocer raged, "Tell those — priests, this time I'm going to call my lawyer and sue them!"

In the 1911/12 school year, Carroll transferred the lowest grades to the new parish school at Immaculate Conception and introduced elective language courses in French and English. His major enterprise, however, was to build a new home for the college. Ideas were explored for an expansion of Garrand's building but these proved impractical. Then plans were drawn up to erect a new building next to the original church at St. Joseph's, to which end Carroll launched an ambitious fund raising drive with lay leadership.

Armed with a massive frame and a commanding voice, Carroll was accustomed to pushing aside every obstacle, but he could not overcome financial reality and the Seattle Diocese's opposition to any expensive Jesuit migrations. Such resistance may seem selfish, but Jesuits and the Diocese had to tap the same local resources to finance their respective plans, and the latter was scrambling to keep up with the city's growth. This competition would bring the Jesuits and the Diocese into conflict more than once.

The college program struggled for students and credibility. In 1910, a master of arts degree was granted to James R. Daly, a part-time instructor at the college (more rigorous standards precluded additional postgraduate degrees for many years after this). Four men took their bachelors of arts degree in a commencement ceremony at the Moore Theatre in June 1913.

The following school year, William O'Connell, who later became editor of the *Catholic Northwest Progress*, was elected president of the first student body association, and regular publication of a yearbook, named *Palestra* after the Greek gymnasium for wrestlers, was launched in 1914. This was Father Carroll's last year as president, but he didn't move far: he became Immaculate Conception's first independent pastor. This separation of duties relieved future college presidents of responsibility for the parish.

The new president, Father Joseph Tomkin, SJ, arrived in the summer of 1914 from Los Angeles College (Loyola Marymount today), which he had helped found three years before. Tomkin "did nothing by halves," in the phrase of one historian, and moved quickly to complete Carroll's reforms by transferring out the rest of the school's younger students and by organizing

As pictured in the 1909 Annual, the recipients of Seattle College's first baccalaureate degrees: John Concannon, John Ford, and Theodore Ryan.

Overleaf: When Seattle College relocated to the Interlaken Boulevard campus of a defunct Swedish Baptist academy in 1919, it was a college in name only.

Inset: Seattle College's love affair with basketball was in full bloom by 1923.

six of the eleven faculty members into the first College of Arts and Sciences.

Tomkin recognized that the times were changing and put more emphasis on the science courses which began to displace classical languages and other traditional elements of the *Ratio Studiorum*. These improvements might have energized college enrollment, which had yet to exceed two dozen, but the outbreak of war in Europe mounted overwhelming competition in the form of high-paying jobs in Seattle's booming defense industries. The sudden exodus of older students from classrooms to shipyards prompted one member of the faculty to quip ruefully, "It is a saying that Seattle Dry Dock and Construction, one of the largest ship building

plants in the country, is run by Seattle College."

America's entry into the conflict on April 6, 1917, dealt another blow to the college program as patriotic students raced to recruiting offices. President Woodrow Wilson delivered the coup de grace in May 1918 when he organized Student Army Training Corps at selected universities. Seattle College lacked such a program, and most of its remaining students transferred to Gonzaga which had trained cadets since 1909.

After awarding degrees to the college's two remaining seniors in June 1918, Tomkin ran up the white flag and ordered an "indefinite continuance" of the college program. The Spanish Flu struck Seattle that fall and closed Seattle College and every other school until November.

IV

DETOUR ON INTERLAKEN

ather Tomkin was overdue for some good luck when he received a call from Father John McHugh, SJ, pastor of St. Joseph's, and Thomas C. McHugh (no relation) on the evening of Monday, February 21, 1919. They had a little proposition.

T.C. McHugh was a wealthy entrepreneur and a devout Catholic. When he sold his interest in the Deep Sea Cannery Company the previous year, he made "a promise to God" to give $50,000 to charity. In fulfilling his pledge, he sought out the counsel of Father McHugh, who suggested that he might help poor, struggling Seattle College. While T. C. McHugh was considering this, he heard on the business grapevine that Adelphia College's mortgage had been foreclosed and the property could be had for the proverbial song.

Adelphia occupied a seven acre tract on Interlaken Boulevard with a spectacular view of Portage Bay and a curious history. In 1884, it had caught the eye of Seattle's second permanent priest, Father Emmanuel Demanez, who persuaded the Diocese to purchase fourteen acres in 1884 for a new cemetery. Church leaders later decided that it was "too far out" from the city center and when Bishop Junger couldn't make the payments, the property was sold. Bishop O'Dea then reconsidered and repurchased the site, but after a few burials at his new Holy Cross Cemetery, he decided it was "too close in" to the city center. In truth, the

land proved so soggy that the city ordered the cemetery closed for health reasons. The few remains interred there were relocated to the new Calvary Cemetery.

In 1905, a Dr. Schmidt appeared on the scene and purchased the swampy tract. Schmidt headed a group of Swedish Baptists with ambitious plans for a college and seminary. They sold half of the acreage and raised or borrowed $100,000 for two modern halls and extensive landscaping. The school survived less than a decade (reportedly the victim of internal dissension) and defaulted on a $45,000 mortgage held by Title Trust of New York and the local Scandinavian Bank.

T. C. McHugh learned that the banks were entertaining a $75,000 offer, a third of the campus's true value, from the Assembly of Seattle Baptist Churches, but no deal had been reached. This was the news he and Father McHugh breathlessly imparted to Father Tomkin as they bundled him and his assistant, Father Burke,

into a car shortly before 9 p.m. on February 21. Once at Adelphia, they "walked down to see the piece." How much they could discern on a winter night is debatable, but it was more than enough to convince all four that this must be Seattle College's next home.

Four days later, T. C. McHugh offered the banks $65,000 in cash and short-term pledges. He hoped other benefactors would help with the purchase, but as Tomkin later wrote with more than a little sarcasm, "Seattle, true to her traditions, would not come forward." So McHugh consulted with his wife, took out a hefty life insurance policy to protect his family, and disposed of his war bonds and other liquid assets in order to plunk down $50,000.

Only the paperwork remained to be completed when the provincial superior, and former College President, Father Dillon, arrived from Portland on March 1 to review the transaction. He immediately approved, which was good because rumors of what the college was up to had already set off howls of protests from the Diocese. It did not welcome a Jesuit school suddenly transplanting itself into the middle of another parish without invitation or warning.

Bishop O'Dea went so far as to consult the national Apostolic Delegate while his staff tried to talk T.C. McHugh out of the transaction. O'Dea even suggested a "compromise" by which the Jesuits would give St. Joseph's Parish — the wealthiest in the city — to the Diocese in

Seattle College ended a seven-year hiatus in 1925 by awarding bachelors of arts degrees to Howard LeClair, Henry Ivers, and George Stuntz (far right).

exchange for his blessing for the new campus. Dillon stood his ground and signed the final purchase documents on March 12.

The Seattle Diocese took a little longer to reconcile itself to the fait accompli, but it did eventually accept it and Bishop O'Dea presided personally over the dedication of Seattle College's new campus on December 7, 1919. Reflecting on these events, Father Tomkin later wrote, "The gift came at our darkest hour, when it seemed that we could only pray and hope for better days. I am firmly convinced that the holy deceased Fathers who toiled here years ago brought 'God's own time' most unexpectedly."

After some frantic cleaning and remodeling during the summer, Seattle College welcomed 143 students to its new Interlaken Campus in September 1919. This left the problem of what to do with the old Broadway Campus. When desultory attempts to sell the property produced no buyers, the college offered it rent-free to the Knights of Columbus. This organization already possessed an imposing hall, built only a block away in 1913, but it wanted additional space for a new series of evening programs for World War I veterans. The Knights paid $200 for the salvage value of the old WCTU house and tore it down. They used Garrand's building off and on, but largely abandoned the site to the weeds and vandals.

The idea of Jesuit higher education remained dormant for the moment. Seattle College had all but legally appended "High School" to its name when its preparatory instruction received official state accreditation in 1921. That summer, Father Geoffrey O'Shea, SJ, (who had served briefly as Immaculate Conception's interim pastor in 1914) transferred from his Gonzaga professorship to succeed Tomkin, who, in turn, later became a trustee of Gonzaga. Such musical chairs became common between the two school's faculties, despite the fierce rivalry of their respective student bodies.

The following year, O'Shea began to reconstruct the "college" in Seattle College's name by introducing a two-year program. In 1923, a third year was added and then a fourth. Thanks to some sophomores who transferred from Gonzaga, Seattle College was able to grant three baccalaureate degrees on June 10, 1925. The recipients were Henry T. Ivers, Howard LeClair, and George Stuntz, who would all play roles in the future life of their alma mater. These three new bachelors of arts were the first since 1918. Although they brought the school's grand total of college graduates to only 30, it marked a new beginning for Seattle College.

O'Shea left Seattle shortly after the 1925 commencement for new duties in Yakima, and Father William Boland, SJ, motored up from Tacoma's St. Leo's parish to take his place. Boland's chief concern was nurturing the college-level courses, which attracted fewer than two dozen in the 1926/27 session. These scant recruits must have withstood a lot of hazing about going to college at a "high school." Indeed, at that time, the bustling University of Washington campus across the Montlake Cut, included some 700 professed Catholics who studied with their backs turned away from the struggling Jesuit college to the south.

A s a first step in elevating the college's status, Boland separated administration of the preparatory and college programs and installed Father Edward McNamara, SJ, as the first principal of the former. When college enrollment actually dropped to nineteen the following year, Boland and his trustees decided that only a complete physical separation could save the college from being totally eclipsed by the high school.

In the process of trying to accomplish this, Boland and the college became ensnared in a tangled web of real estate propositions, land swaps, and diocesan politics. It began innocently enough early in 1927 when Bishop O'Dea learned that the college was contemplating development of a new campus. He suggested to Boland that he might consider a site near a 50-acre tract in north Seattle which the Diocese had recently purchased. There were also dark hints that if the Jesuits couldn't succeed at higher Catholic education, perhaps the Diocese should take over the effort.

No definite action was taken during the year, but extensive discussion of the problem continued. Over the Christmas holidays, Boland had occasion to talk the matter over with William Pigott, president of Pacific Car and Foundry (now PACCAR) and one of Seattle's most generous supporters of Catholic causes. According to Boland's report to his provincial, Father Joseph Piet, SJ, Pigott thought colleges were "useless," but he did support high schools, and Pigott later offered to help finance an expansion of the Interlaken campus.

This was not what Boland needed. He was set on a new campus, but his plans depended on selling the original Broadway site. The lack of buyers led Piet to scold Boland in February 1928, "The Broadway situation is certainly annoying." Piet planned to investigate the matter

Fr. Geoffrey O'Shea, SJ, rebuilt the "college" in Seattle College's name. (OPA)

Thomas C. McHugh heard that Adelphia's campus was for sale and ended up buying it for Seattle College. (Courtesy of Charles McHugh)

Fr. William Boland, SJ, lamented, "The college affair here seems to whirl year after year in some kind of vicious circle."

Fr. Joseph Tomkin, SJ, paid a nighttime visit to Adelphia College and liked what little he could see. (OPA)

William Pigott (above) thought colleges were "useless" but pledged to help buy a new campus anyway (Courtesy of Ann Wyckoff). Fr. Walter Fitzgerald, SJ, (far right) traded away Immaculate Conception Parish for a new North End campus and then the stock market crashed (OPA). Fr. John McHugh, SJ, briefly took charge of the college in 1931 and sent it back to Broadway "temporarily." (OPA)

personally after he returned from Father Cataldo's Diamond Jubilee in Spokane, but his schedule was interrupted by an unforeseen tragedy.

An automobile accident a month after this celebration of Cataldo's seventy-fifth year as a Jesuit claimed the pioneering missionary's life. Cataldo, who had traversed the Pacific Northwest by horse, wagon, river raft, steamboat, locomotive, and most of all, on foot, was brought down by a missed curve on the road to Pendleton and died April 9, 1928.

Once the shock of such a loss had passed, Piet and his colleagues returned to the business of the Province and its disparate institutions. The situation at Seattle College took a new turn for the worse when a fire damaged the Jesuit residence at Interlaken in July. That same month, Father Walter Fitzgerald, SJ, representing Piet, met with Bishop O'Dea to review Seattle College's needs. A 40-acre tract at 32nd Avenue Northeast and Northeast 70th Street had been identified, near the Benedictine's new Assumption parish. Fitzgerald proposed that the Jesuits trade the Immaculate Conception parish for Assumption and develop their new college in the north end, and the Bishop concurred pending the Benedictine's approval.

After a month of no action, Boland lamented to Piet, "The college affair here seems to whirl year after year in some kind of vicious circle. We haven't adequate classes because we

haven't the professors. And we haven't the professors because we haven't the classes. The truth is we haven't the boys."

Father McHugh added a new twist in August when he came forward with another site, the 38-acre "Thorpe" property at 35th Northeast and Northeast 85th. At this point there were more properties and dollars on the table than in a game of Monopoly, but all parties agreed on the Thorpe site. Father Boland reached for his "chance card," and William Pigott agreed to finance purchase of the Thorpe site while the Jesuits agreed to surrender Immaculate Conception for the northern portion of Assumption Parish.

Boland made the down payment with $1,000 provided by Pigott. A few days later, Pigott died — before he could provide for the $64,000 balance in his will. The college was trapped in an exchange of parishes for a campus which it could not afford. Things were so desperate by November 1928, one Jesuit lamented in the official community diary, "We have done everything possible to raise the money necessary to close the deal, except rob a bank. Yet we are told to go on."

And so they did. In the summer of 1929, with no funds for a new campus, Boland rented a duplex at 921 Roanoke East to give his 21 college students at least the illusion of separation from the high school, although they had to hike from their "Roanoke Campus" to use the library and laboratories on Interlaken.

Boland left for new duties in Santa Barbara and was succeeded on September 4 by the same Father Fitzgerald who had helped to engineer the north end acquisition. The Jesuits remodeled a log cabin as a chapel for their new St. Ignatius Parish in north Seattle. A deal was a deal, and on September 23, 1929, diocese chancellor Monsignor Theodore Ryan, one of Seattle College's three original graduates, took the keys to Immaculate Conception Parish from his former Jesuit teachers. A month later, on October 25, 1929 — "Black Friday" — the stock market collapsed, crushing any dreams for developing a new parish and campus.

Fitzgerald was a former rector and president of Gonzaga and he was destined to become Bishop of Alaska. Armed with proven skills as an administrator, he had more than a passing knowledge of events to date at Seattle College. Fitzgerald toted up the Jesuits' debts, which came to $154,000, and took stock of his domain, whose real estate value more than exceeded his liabilities, at least on paper. As the full impact of the Great Depression began to be felt, Fitzgerald wisely decided to stand pat.

Dreams of a new campus were held in abeyance while Fitzgerald presided over the graduation of three college seniors in June 1930. Following a record enrollment of 30 in September, Fitzgerald took the calculated risk of inviting an accreditation by the University of Washington that December. He knew Seattle College would fail to meet state standards, but he hoped that the evaluation might spur support for necessary improvements.

The accreditation report had barely arrived on Fitzgerald's desk when he learned that he was to head the new Rocky Mountain division of the province, embracing the entire Pacific Northwest and Alaska. On February 10, 1931, his seat as president of the college was taken by none other than Father McHugh, who had played such an enormous role in the college's fortunes as pastor of St. Joseph's, a position he retained.

With both the high school and the rented "Roanoke Campus" filled to the rafters and with development of the north end properties now foreclosed by the deepening Depression, McHugh played the only card left in his hand: he would send his struggling college program back to its birthplace on Broadway "temporarily."

Babe Ruth demonstrates what made him the "Sultan of Swat" during a 1925 visit to the Interlaken Campus. (OPA)

While Seattle College struggled on Interlaken, hundreds of Catholics enrolled at the U of W just across Portage Bay.

Overleaf: Giant letters along the parapet of the Garrand Building announced in 1931 that Seattle College had come home.

Inset: Fr. James McGoldrick, SJ, defied authority and convention in the 1930s to pioneer Jesuit co-education at Seattle College.

V

BACK TO BROADWAY

The first Jesuit to return to the old campus was Father Louis Egan, SJ. What he found was not a pretty sight. Garrand's once imposing edifice was blighted with broken windows and cracked masonry, and its upper floors still bore the scars of the 1907 fire. The dilapidated building was surrounded by an overgrown field choked with weeds and littered with trash.

Egan's mission was to turn this urban eyesore into a functioning college by September. He estimated that minimum repairs would cost $15,000 and Fitzgerald quickly raised the money while the Jesuits, students and their friends set to work sweeping, weeding and rebuilding through the summer. The money and time stretched only as far as the third story (the top floor was not renovated until 1936) but the college was ready by Sunday, September 13, 1931.

On that day Monsignor Ryan presided over the rededication attended by faculty, well-wishers and students. Above their heads, giant block letters along the parapet built by Garrand thirty-seven years before announced the news to the city: Seattle College had come home.

On Monday, 46 students arrived for classes, a record enrollment that included 31 freshmen. They were greeted by five Jesuits: Fathers Howard F. Peronteau, dean of the college department; Daniel J. Reidy, a former president of Gonzaga who taught philosophy; Raymond A. Nichols, professor of history and economics;

James B. McGoldrick, professor of psychology; and John Prange, professor of physics. Their academic titles understated the incredible scope of their knowledge and versatility as educators, administrators and energetic innovators. They *were* the college.

Of these first five, one man was perhaps more equal than the others, Father McGoldrick. Born August 15, 1895, in County Sligo, Ireland, McGoldrick was the fourth of twelve children. He was impressed by Jesuits as a child and resolved to enter the Society, which he did in 1918. McGoldrick soon mastered Latin, Greek and French, but he dreamed of joining the Jesuit pioneers in Alaska and volunteered for the Rocky Mountain Mission. He got half of his wish in 1920 when he was assigned to Gonzaga College. There he finished his studies as a scholastic, earning both his bachelor's and master's degrees, and became Dean of the School of Education before his ordination in 1930.

The closest McGoldrick ever came to Alaska

was Seattle, where he was assigned to help reopen the college. Slight, already balding and with a mischievous twinkle behind his wire-rimmed spectacles, he brought a quick humor and lilting Irish brogue to the school and soon became everyone's favorite.

Students dubbed McGoldrick, Peronteau, Nichols and Reidy the "Four Horsemen of Loyola," with Prange as their able "backup." It was apt, because these men charged into the business of reviving the dream of Seattle College with unstinting and infectious enthusiasm. They didn't worry about breaking any rules in the process, and that landed them in trouble almost immediately.

The nation's economy continued to deteriorate, but unlike the Panic of 1893, bad times actually helped the college in one respect. The forced idleness of so many Catholic workers and the urgency felt by others to improve their job skills created a new demand for higher education. Thanks to its low tuition, only $25 a quarter, so many applicants came knocking on Seattle College's door that Father McGoldrick organized a new evening "extension school." This program promptly enrolled 79 students in 1931 — including women, who joined their male counterparts in the same classes, effectively making Seattle College co-educational.

Most of these female students, it should be noted, were nuns who had no other place to turn for Catholic higher education, but nuns or

Seattle College was beginning to look, sound and act like a real college as new students, faculty and equipment were squeezed into the college hall. A bookstore opened in the basement of the Garrand building, Peronteau organized a debating society, and the college's first basketball team took to the boards in the Knights of Columbus gymnasium.

On January 9, 1933, students published their first newspaper, *Theatas*, meaning "Spectator" in Greek. The four mimeographed pages were barely legible, but the dedicated reader could decipher the news that the admission price for the winter informal dance "is in accord with the present-day depression," a new radio had been installed in the smoking room, and a "skid road gospel slinger" [sic] had briefly invaded the college before being expelled.

Founding *Spectator* editor Vincent Gerhardt also emphasized that Seattle College and the high school were separate institutions. The second and subsequent weekly issues begged, "When is the high school going to change its name?" (This wish was not granted until December 7, 1933, when the Interlaken Campus officially became Seattle Preparatory School.)

In June 1933, the college awarded three baccalaureate degrees and fourteen junior college certificates. That fall, alumni pitched in to help revive their old college's life. Father Concannon ('09), Henry Ivers, and Howard LeClair (both '25) organized a drama society and staged the school's first production, *Stop Thief*, in October 1933.

By the November 9 issue of the *Spectator*—all pretense to ancient Greek was dropped the previous March and the paper found a decent printer—a student complained about male dominance of athletics, "We girls feel that, in our own way, we are as capable of holding up the laurels of the school as the men." Indeed, with the new school year, Seattle College had also dropped any pretense about its co-educational program.

The "Four Horsemen of Loyola" pose with Fr. Albert Lemieux, SJ, (second from left) in 1948. From left to right: Jesuit Frs. Raymond Nichols, James McGoldrick, Daniel Reidy, and Howard Peronteau.

Fr. John Prange, SJ, proved an able "backup." (OPA)

Fr. Louis Egan, SJ, blazed the trail back to Broadway.

not, co-education was still regarded as a radical innovation. The college's "mixed classes" drew censorious reproofs from Provincial and Diocesan authorities. Peronteau tried to mollify these critics by replying that evening students were not really matriculated in the college, so no rules had been broken. What he neglected to report was the fact that on McGoldrick's watch, "evening" classes began at noon.

The issue simmered without any direct intervention in the college's affairs. The following June, as the college prepared to award two baccalaureate degrees in ceremonies at St. Joseph's, Peronteau received the happy news that the University of Washington had accredited its junior college program (endorsement of the full four-year program would come five years later).

By the time the 1932 school year was ready to commence, Seattle had reached its economic nadir. The college's cash reserves had dwindled from thousands of dollars to nearly nothing. Reluctantly, the trustees raised the tuition to $35 per quarter. The hike did not discourage enrollment and 73 students registered for day classes.

Seattle College's Jesuit Community in 1936. (OPA)

Bottom row: Dennis Sullivan, Francis Sansone, Joseph Georgen, (President) John Balfe, James McGoldrick, James McGuigan, Francis Logan, Natalis Maruca.

Second row: John O'Brien, John Concannon, Gerald McDonald, Clifford Carroll, Clair Marshall, Gerald Beezer, Arthur Flajole, Leo Schmid.

Third row: Maurice Meagher, Donald McDonald, Daniel Reidy, Howard Peronteau, Raymond Nichols, Louis St. Marie, Anthony Bischoff, Joseph Nealen.

Top row: Gerard Evoy, Robert Dachy, Louis Geiss, Edward Keenan, Harold Greif.

Fr. John Balfe, SJ, greets visiting students from Tokyo's Sophia University. Fr. Leo Schmid, SJ, (below) inventories his specimens. If the supply is low, neighborhood pets beware!

McGoldrick, now dean of the faculty, later recalled, "In my early years it was held that women couldn't grasp metaphysics or advanced mathematics — I heard university professors claim that. And I understood it was folly, because my own sisters were experts in math, and they could beat any of us in philosophy." As to breaking Society rules, he added, "My opinion prevailed [that] it wasn't that our constitution forbids women to be educated, it was just never before considered."

As head of the new Oregon Province and a former president of the college, Father Fitzgerald tolerated co-education, telling McGoldrick, "I can't give you permission, but I won't block you." Seattle's new bishop, Gerald Shaughnessy (O'Dea had died Christmas Day, 1932) was not so liberal. Neither was Rome, to which Shaughnessy protested. McGoldrick's response to all critics was blunt: if he had to choose between men and women, "Then I'll dismiss the boys." The college's new president, Father John Balfe, SJ, offered a more diplomatic but no less firm defense when Superior General Wlodimir Ledochowski enquired from Rome in 1934.

Balfe carefully explained that expulsion of women would reduce the student body below the number required for full accreditation. "We

may order the women students of the Extension School to depart, but, if we do, most of the young men students will depart also, because they will lose confidence in the college..." Because that in turn would probably spell the end of the college once and for all, Balfe implored, "This calamity we must try earnestly to avoid."

Balfe's bottom line was "financial necessity," and it proved persuasive for the moment. The Diocese repeatedly grumbled about women and men studying together at the college, and the Society warned other schools against emulating Seattle, but it did not order McGoldrick to expel his distaff students. The issue was left an uneasy stalemate.

The new academic year of 1935 marked a turning point as more than 500 full-time and extension students enrolled that fall. McGoldrick, fortified with a new doctorate in education from the University of Washington, where he made many influential friends, founded the college's first discrete academic unit, the School of Education. At the same time, Father Clifford Carroll, SJ, organized a department of business education, Charles Braz opened the drama department, and Walter Aklin arranged a music department.

Mrs. E.M. Anna Proutz also joined the school as its first dean of women (she was later succeeded by Marie Leonard who filled this position for many years) and organized a residence hall and lounge in an old house at 10th and Marion. This was better than the Jesuits enjoyed. They still had to commute from their Interlaken residence at Seattle Prep via the college's one and only automobile. Even when the college's ancient Ford ran, which it did not reliably do, it was not always available to shuttle the Jesuits.

This meant shanks' mare more often than not, or the street car. The latter became a public relations vehicle when McGoldrick prevailed upon its conductor to call out "Seattle College" when stopping at Broadway and Madison. The same street car was the scene of near panic when the wrappings fell from a human skeleton being transported to the college by a new faculty member, Father Leo Schmid, SJ.

Schmid laid the foundations for Seattle College's later reputation for excellence in the biological sciences, but limited funds demanded that he beg supplies and castoff equipment from local physicians, whom he regularly canvassed through the telephone directory. His skeletal companion on the street car was the result of one such call. If medical charity lagged behind his needs, Schmid resorted to other means. When his stock of animal specimens for dissection ran low, the *Spectator* and community papers put out the alert: "Neighbors warned to keep pets on leash!"

Schmid conducted at least one additional unscheduled anatomy lesson when his students lost control of a male cadaver they were transporting down the stairs of the Garrand building. The body bumped down the steps and landed naked at the feet of a group of co-eds, who fled shrieking from the hall.

Despite such mishaps, Schmid's efforts allowed the college to launch pre-medical courses. This set the stage for the most important development of the time: establishment of a department of nursing education in conjunction with the Sisters of Providence. Their hospital had already made arrangements with the University of Washington for the education of its student nurses, but it struck Providence's Sister John Gabriel that Seattle College should be the hospital's preferred campus, given both its physical and spiritual proximity. The author of five books, including the ground-breaking *Through the Patient's Eyes* and scores of articles, Sister John Gabriel was a proponent of scientific rigor and psychological sensitivity in the training of nurses, and a natural collaborator with McGoldrick. The new department was an instant success, enrolling 75 nurses in the fall of 1935.

The following May, the college's four-year program received its official seal of approval from the University of Washington, which permitted students to transfer or pursue post-graduate studies with no loss of credits. The next month, Seattle College awarded 21 degrees in ceremonies at Providence Hospital. Among the graduates were eight women, the college's first, and foremost among these was Sister John Gabriel, who received her master of arts.

President Balfe was not present for this occasion. Illness had compelled his departure in February, and Father McHugh guided the college in the interim from St. Joseph's Parish. On June 11, 1936, Father Francis Corkery, SJ, was named as the college's thirteenth rector and, at the age of 33, the nation's youngest college president. His first duty was a happy one: accepting a gift of $10,000 from Mrs. Hermina Hambach. He spent the money rehabilitating the college's fourth floor, which had been closed off since the fire of 1907.

The college needed the room for the 675 students who enrolled that fall. The faculty expanded to 16 Jesuits, one nun, and 19 laymen. Corkery began renting or buying houses in the immediate neighborhood to accommodate the overflow. The college marked another milestone in 1936 by creating a department of social work under direction of Father William J. Walsh and Helen G. Farrell. More innovations followed: the first alumni association reunion or "Homecoming" in November, the first school fight song, the first constitution (of many) for the "Associated Students of Seattle College," (ASSC) and election of its first president, Robert L. Smith. In May 1937, the college yearbook, *Aegis*, made its debut. Edited by Margaret Guest and dedicated to Father McGoldrick, the inaugural *Aegis* previewed a commencement in which women graduates outnumbered men 36 to 26, and its photo gallery featured many students of Philippine and Asian descent.

Seattle College was a real college at last. It was also evolving in ways its founders could never have imagined.

Sister John Gabriel, SP, laid the foundation for the School of Nursing. (SPA)

Fr. Francis Corkery became the 13th president of Seattle College on June 11, 1936.

Overleaf: This 1948 aerial view looks to the southwest over Seattle College's motley campus of war surplus pre-fabs, a former car dealership and cable car barn, a transplanted gymnasium, and converted houses and apartments.

Inset: Students buy "Defense Stamps" to support the war effort. (OPA)

VI

IN WAR AND PEACE

World events were beginning to impinge on campus life. Students staged passionate debates over fascism, communism, capitalism; many preferred "distributivism," an informal set of ideas merging Christian charity and democratic socialism favored by many Catholic intellectuals at the time. The student body also preferred Franklin Roosevelt, "voting" for his 1936 re-election by 83 percent in a straw poll.

Hitler's growing power was a cause of more dissension. Many students agreed with one Church leader that they "were crucified between two thieves, Russia and the Reich." Add the antipathy for Britain felt by students of Irish descent and the sympathy of Italy's sons and daughters for their homeland despite Mussolini, and the isolationism of Seattle College on the eve of the Second World War is more than understandable. As one editorialist in the *Spectator* put it, "Let's just for a change heed our instincts (for survival) and stay out of this whole sordid foreign mess." In truth, most Americans agreed.

For the moment, at least, there were more pressing issues to occupy the students' attention, such as the name of their basketball team. Although victorious more often than not under the coaching of a local dentist, Jim Logan, the Maroons (named for the school colors) were an easy target for opponents' gibes. Weary of being called "morons" or reading about their

"marooned" hoopsters, students demanded a different name for the team. Ed Donohoe, the *Spectator's* ace sports writer and the team's first publicist, came to the rescue with a new moniker: Chieftains.

Donohoe didn't go through any hoops to adopt the new name. He later recalled, "I just started using it." The name, which honored Chief Seattle, was received enthusiastically and became official on January 21, 1938. Donohoe went on to become the editor of the influential *Washington Teamster* where he punctured many a stuffed shirt in his column, "Tilting At Windmills."

Enrollment reached 1,000 the following fall — a 2,200 percent growth in just five years — and Seattle College was bursting at the seams. To house and teach this multitude, Corkery found himself becoming one of Capitol Hill's largest landlords. He acquired the Otis and Marne Hotels (formerly St. Rose's), leased an entire wing of the Sorrento Hotel as a women's

dormitory, shifted classes to the Knights of Columbus hall, and began renting or buying every available house in the vicinity of the campus. These included two once-great mansions which were renamed for the Jesuit heroes Bellarmine and Campion.

Despite, or perhaps because of the crowding, the college developed a special sense of community not found on more spacious campuses. By now, social life was organized into a host of Church-based fraternities and sororities and numerous academic clubs. One of the first and longest-surviving of these was the hiking group called Hiyu Coolee (or "Cole") after the Chinook jargon for "much walk." The club's first expedition was an eight-mile trek on February 22, 1939, from West Seattle's Lincoln Park to Three Tree Point, led by Father Francis Logan, SJ, who had just arrived on campus as a new instructor in French.

The college's ragtag real estate empire was still not enough to house the growing enrollment. Corkery launched a $200,000 fund drive for a new Liberal Arts Building, which Bishop Shaughnessy graciously agreed to chair despite his criticisms of college policies. To design the new building, the college retained John Maloney, a young architect who went on to plan most of the college and the Diocese's future construction. He chose a streamlined gothic style with a central tower topped by an octagonal belfry reminiscent of the one with which Garrand had

Fr. Francis Logan, SJ, remains fit 50 years after he started the Hiyu Coolees, who would go from alpine hiking to hop-harvesting during World War II.

Students jam into "The Cave" on the eve of the war.

capped the college's first building almost a half-century earlier.

Ground was broken on October 18, 1940, but excavation of the foundation halted almost immediately after it began when workers unearthed a mass of bones of unknown origin. Both archaeologists and homicide detectives descended on the scene. Fortunately, Father Schmid was around to explain the mystery: the diggers had stumbled upon the burial ground for his biological specimens.

Another old issue was unearthed in 1940 when the highest ranking Jesuit in the United States came into possession of that year's *Aegis*. Father Zacheus Maher, SJ, complained bitterly to the new Oregon Provincial, Father William Elliott, SJ, "The whole book is so completely a girl's book that I wonder if the editors have given a thought to how much pain it would cause His Paternity [the Superior General in Rome] were it ever to reach him." Maher continued, "Dances, dances, dances, girls sports, basketball for girls, bowling for girls...all these in the name of Jesuit education..."

When Maher later came to Seattle to help dedicate the new Liberal Arts Building, he bearded McGoldrick in his den of co-educational iniquity. McGoldrick wasn't intimidated, and told his visitor sharply, "That's settled and I'm not reopening the question." As McGoldrick recalled later, "Zac became as quiet as a mouse." The issue was indeed settled, although the Society would not formally accept co-education until 1948. Thus, Seattle helped to blaze the co-educational trail for all Jesuit colleges.

One final matter was laid to rest in 1940: the Jesuits abandoned their St. Ignatius Parish to the Diocese, which reorganized it as Our Lady of the Lake Parish. The would-be north end campus was sold the following year for $20,000, less than a third of its original price.

As work on the new Liberal Arts Building progressed into 1941, Corkery realized that he was not going to raise the full cost of construc-

tion (despite another $30,000 gift from Mrs. Hambach). He decided to postpone finishing the interior of the south wing but limited funds did not prevent him from snatching up a bargain when he saw one. On April 21, 1941, Corkery paid $9,000 for the old Madison Street cable car terminal as a home for the new School of Engineering then being organized by Father Edmund McNulty, SJ.

A brilliant and energetic professor of science, McNulty had founded Gonzaga College's engineering department in 1934 by exploiting the demand for engineers created by construction of the nearby Grand Coulee Dam. This innovation was widely credited with saving Gonzaga's fortunes in the depths of the Depression, yet the new Jesuit Education Association opposed Seattle College's plan for a comparable department. As in the matter of co-education, the college was undaunted, but the JEA did block McGoldrick's plans for a law school. The aptly named Professor Henry Drill served as acting Dean of the School of Engineering when it opened in fall 1941, but McNulty soon took over and remained its driving force for the rest of his long career at the college. Also that fall, the former department of nursing became a full-fledged School of Nursing under the direction of Dr. Harry Shaw, MD.

The Liberal Arts Building was finished, or more accurately, half-finished, and dedicated on June 22, 1941, in time for the registration of almost 1,500 full- and part-time students for the 1941/42 academic year. All of them found their way sooner or later to the new eatery and lounge in the former gym in the basement of the Science Building, as Garrand's venerable pile was then called. The "College Cavern" was soon dubbed simply "The Cave" and became the social center for the entire campus community.

The year was off to a great start, and Seattle College, once deemed the least likely to succeed, now ranked as Washington State's third largest institution of higher education.

Corkery and his colleagues could be forgiven if they thought that the college had finally arrived. After all, what could possibly go wrong?

On December 7, 1941, Japan attacked the Pacific Fleet at Pearl Harbor, and the United States found itself in the war. Until this point many had thought the nation could stay out of "this whole sordid foreign mess," but the signs had not been good for some time.

Back in the fall of 1940, 30 students, along with Father McGoldrick, had volunteered for flying lessons sponsored by the Civil Aviation Administration and intended to prepare reserve pilots for the military. The first of these students to earn his wings, Lt. John Geis, died when his Army Air Corps bomber crashed during a training run in February 1941. The situation in Europe took on additional vividness as Edith Strauss, a Jewish student, horrified her fellow students with her tale of narrowly escaping Hitler's concentration camps.

By March 1941, the city had begun conducting practice blackouts, and in April, Edward J. Fujiwara became the first college student inducted under the limited draft instituted the previous October. By fall, the *Spectator* could still crack a weak joke about "shorter skirts for national defense — war is the greatest fashion designer this season," but it was gallows humor. When the nation's call came after Pearl Harbor, 250 Seattle College students promptly enlisted, and male enrollment plummeted until women outnumbered men on campus by six to one.

The war came home in other ways as Japanese-Americans were rounded up for internment. The college bade farewell to many beloved students and staff members, whom it protected against anti-Japanese bigotry until the last detainees departed for camps isolated from the Pacific Coast. On January 23, 1942, Father Corkery announced that the college was now on a "war footing" under which it would accelerate instruction to four quarters a year and accept high school seniors in the summer after gradua-

Fr. Edmund McNulty, SJ, founded the School of Engineering in time to supply technicians for the war effort, but remodeling the former Madison Street cable car building for engineering classes had to wait for the war's end.

tion. He suspended the yearbook and non-essential programs.

Everyone did his or her part for the war effort. Corkery joined the powerful War Labor Board which directed labor relations and set wages throughout the Northwest and Alaska. The university stepped forward in February 1942 to help the government reactivate Army Base Hospital Number 50, a reserve combat medical unit dormant since the First World War. Col. Hubbard Buckner, M.D., a long-time supporter of the college's pre-med program and a veteran of the first base hospital, was named commander and Coralee Steele became charge nurse for 120 women recruited from Seattle College and Providence Hospital.

In September 1942, the "Fighting 50th" was sent for training to Colorado (in part because Washington had no medical school at the time) and then to active duty in England. It ultimately followed Allied troops into Normandy shortly after D-Day 1944 where it established a 1500-bed medical center, one of the war's largest, just behind the front lines. The unit earned the Citation of Merit for its tireless care of tens of thousands of wounded soldiers. (The 50th general hospital unit was mobilized for the 1991 Persian Gulf War, but without university involvement.)

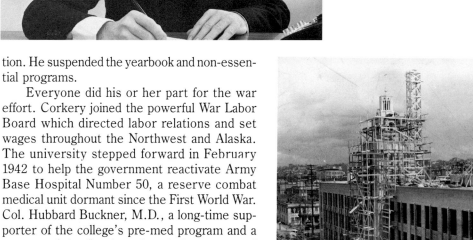

After solving the mystery of the skeletons, workers speed completion of the Administration Building.

Fr. Corkery visits Col. Hubbard Buckner, MD, to review plans for Seattle University's hospital corps.

General Hospital #50 chaplain James Gilmore, SJ, on the front.

Seattle University nurses troop the colors at the end of their training in Colorado.

Students served the nation in other ways. Because the war had reduced the ranks of farm workers, the Hiyu Coolees traveled to Wenatchee to pick apples and later to Yakima to help bring in the hops. Engineering and science students were exempted from the draft to help design and build new weapons, and the college began to forge its first ties with the Boeing Airplane Company, whose *Spectator* advertisements trumpeted, "College Students Help Build the Boeing B-29 Superfortress" for $185 a month.

The war wasn't all work and sacrifice. Regular "Trolley Dances," so called because students were urged to leave their cars at home to save fuel, attracted many even if the shortage of males meant that the girls mostly had to dance with each other. A young pre-law student, Fred Dore (now State Supreme Court Justice) energized the Gavel Club, whose members visited McNeil Island federal prison for a debate. The inmate team, which included two attorneys, clobbered the college but the prisoners appreciated the mental exercise nonetheless. As the students left for the mainland, their hosts told them, "We hope you will come to see us again, but we hope you won't have to stay."

During the spring, John Ayres and Jim Layman "battled" for the 1943 ASSC presidency. The former presented himself as "Dependable, Loyal, Honest" while the latter campaigned as "Honest, Loyal, Dependable." A hard choice but Layman triumphed. Being exempt from the draft, he had the winning slogan: "Elect a man who is sure of returning next fall."

Not everyone did return. The first Seattle College alumnus to fall in combat was Army Sgt. Joseph John Dobler, who graduated in economics in 1937 and died in the Solomon Islands in October 1943. The *Spectator* reported a strange coincidence: a Navy Lt. J.J. Dobler, who had attended Seattle College in 1938 and 1939, also died in the same battle. In all, more than 1,000 Seattle College students and recent graduates served in the armed forces. Some 60 earned

McHugh Hall's 520-gallon bathtub was a prominent campus "fixture" well into the 1960s, when students mugged for this photograph.

Fr. Harold Small, SJ, took over as president in 1945 and braced for an invading army of returning veterans.

commendations for bravery and 27 gave their lives. None of these sacrifices affected the campus more than the death of Anthony Buhr, a popular student who had served as ASSC president in 1942. He fell in the Battle of Leyte in December 1944, while redeeming General Mac Arthur's pledge to return to the Philippines.

The war in Europe ended in May 1945 and veterans began returning to Seattle College. They organized a club in the spring of 1945 and debated the issue of releasing interned Japanese-Americans while fighting continued in the Pacific. Most veterans supported the idea and they were shocked that many Seattleites did not agree with them. One veteran summarized their feelings, "I didn't expect to come back and find such things as race hatred." The issue became moot in August 1945 with the atomic bombings of Hiroshima and Nagasaki.

Father Corkery was not on campus to celebrate V-J Day on September 2, 1945. He was settling into his duties as president of Gonzaga, where he had been assigned the previous April.

The new president of Seattle College was Father Harold Small, SJ, who had attained the position by a political accident.

Born in Missoula near the site of DeSmet's original Northwest Mission, Small joined the Jesuit novitiate after his sixteenth birthday. After taking his doctorate in sociology at Fordham in 1943, Small succeeded Father McGoldrick as Seattle College's dean of studies. This freed McGoldrick to devote himself to his classroom work and to his ardent advocacy of educational reform. Although popular and effective on campus, Small was not the first choice to succeed Corkery. In fact, Oregon Provincial Father Leopold Robinson, SJ, (who succeeded Elliott in 1942) gave the nod to Father Arthur Dussault, SJ, a popular instructor and former football hero at Gonzaga and later its vice-president. When Corkery and the Gonzagans learned of the appointment they complained all the way to Father Maher that Dussault was indispensible in Spokane.

Thus, Father Small suddenly found himself

president of Seattle College at the age of 37. Small's appointment was greeted with great enthusiasm by McGoldrick and his colleagues in the social sciences who hoped for a more sympathetic ear from the new president. Small did not serve long enough to fulfill all their expectations, but he left a major mark on the campus.

The first wave of returning veterans quickly lifted enrollment to over 900 full-time and 300 part-time students when the school year opened in the fall of 1945. A year later, this stream swelled into a tidal wave of almost 2,500, of whom 60 percent were subsidizing their education through the new G.I. Bill. Small was facing an invading army and a logistical nightmare that might have unnerved General Eisenhower. He quickly finished the Liberal Arts Building's south wing and scrambled to buy more real estate in the neighborhood.

Small's first acquisitions were Sarazin Hall at 18th and East Spring and a mansion at 718 Minor built in 1897 by Alfred Anderson, a tim-

Millie Russell, nee Bown, broke down barriers for minorities and women by pursuing a career in clinical science. (Courtesy of Millie Russell)

Faculty members such as Fr. Gerald Beezer, SJ, had no tolerance for intolerance.

Fr. Ray Nichols, SJ, worked with Fugitaro Kubota to beautify the campus and earned the nickname "Father Greengrass."

ber magnate. His widow, Agnes Healy Anderson, insisted on horse drawn transportation long after the advent of the automobile, and her carriage was a familiar sight around the college for decades. She willed her estate to her faithful coachman, from whom the college purchased the house in 1946. The mansion was renamed in honor of Father McHugh, who had died in 1940, and its colossal 520-gallon bathtub was a popular fixture with many generations of students.

The next addition to the campus was the so-called "Savidge Block" immediately east of the Liberal Arts Building. Small cleared the site (except for a large car garage and showroom which survived until the Pigott Building was built) in anticipation of receiving prefabricated barracks made available as surplus from the military under the Mead Act. These arrived from Kirkland in May 1946. The largest, an L-shaped affair with a central heating plant at the corner was named Lyons Hall and later renamed Veteran's Hall. It soon housed 72 men in the college's first on-campus student residence. Smaller prefabs were named in memory of fallen students, Charles Dougherty, Anthony Buhr and Robert Simmons, and used for engineering and art classes. Of these only Vet's heating plant (now used as a foundry under the direction of Professor Marvin Herard) and Buhr Hall remain.

Small's triumph was Memorial Gymnasium, which had been sawed into 16-foot sections and trucked from Paine Field to the east side of 11th Avenue between Marion and Spring. It was reassembled and equipped with bleachers for 1,800 spectators. It was standing room only on December 5, 1947, when the Chieftains inaugurated the stadium with a basketball game against the University of British Columbia. Seattle lost 59 to 58 in a heartbreaker.

The task of making Small's potluck campus appear presentable fell to Father Ray Nichols, who had already earned the nickname "Father Greengrass." He was assisted by Fugitaro Kubota, now free from the internment camps, whose delicate landscaping touches still grace the campus. Kubota's elaborate gardens in South Seattle are now preserved as a city park bearing his name. Asian-Americans were also returning to Seattle College as students and a growing number of foreign-born students, particularly from the Philippines, began to matriculate as the world returned to something resembling normality.

The first significant numbers of African-Americans (judging from photographs in the *Aegis*) also began to enroll. Among them were Lillie Mae Parker, Wyoming Brooks and Sam Smith, who went on to become one of Seattle's longest-serving City Councilmen. Millie Russell (nee Bown and now Assistant Vice President of Minority Affairs at the U of W) made campus news in 1946 when she was named a junior delegate to the NAACP convention in New Orleans. Her experiences offer some sense of what African-Americans encountered at Seattle University.

Russell was raised in a politically active Catholic family; her mother helped found the St. Peter Claver Center for social services in the Immaculate Conception Parish. When Russell announced her ambition to become a nun, Father McGoldrick advised her to go to college first. She recalls, "Some of the priests were not as sensitive to [racial] difference as they should be," but "Father Small was always there for me."

Financial help was provided by the college's long-time registrar, Ruth Brand Johnson, but the greatest influence was exercised by Father Gerald Beezer, SJ. As head of the chemistry department, he recognized Russell's scientific aptitude and steered her toward a degree in medical technology. In helping both an African-American and a woman to pursue such a non-traditional career, Russell notes, Seattle College was far more progressive at that time than most public universities. In 1947, the campus hosted the first of several visits from A. Phillips Randolph, the great union organizer and champion of civil rights. He spoke on labor relations, a field in which the college was developing a reputation thanks to the extra-curricular efforts of Father Robert Carmody, SJ, who was also head of the English department and athletic director. Seattle College's reputation in labor-management arbitration was later extended by Dr. Charles LaCugna, the college's first professor (now emeritus) of political science.

In 1947, the college established a formal School of Commerce and Finance under the direction of Dr. Paul Volpe, who served as dean for almost two decades. The college's faculty had expanded to 32 Jesuits, one nun, and 74 lay men and women. Thanks particularly to the leadership of Fathers Small and McGoldrick, almost 60 percent of these professors and instructors held advanced degrees, an average greater than most public colleges.

Student life was also picking up as the Cave was enlarged and its menu expanded. If it was too crowded, students could go off campus to the nearby "Chieftain" cafeteria (not to be confused with the current student union building) across Madison or The Cottage on 15th Avenue. Or they could grab a bite from John Suga who dispensed treats from his red and white candy truck on the edge of campus. Despite the end of the war, Suga still rationed his stock because, he said, "Too much fun is no good."

There was little risk of Seattle College students overindulging themselves. A *Spectator* survey of students in the summer of 1947 found that 100 percent were employed, with unmarried students earning an average of $112 per month and married couples making $195. The number of the latter was growing dramatically, as evidenced by the long list of wedding announcements which replaced the *Spectator's* wartime "Uncle Sam's College Men" column. For those not yet engaged, campus clubs and

Dr. Charles LaCugna (right), the university's first professor of political science, chats with Senator Henry Jackson and State Attorney General Don Eastwold (far left) in 1955.

Charles Moriarty, an "SC" alum, became Seattle University's "family lawyer."

John Maloney designed the Administration Building and many more campus and church facilities.

Overleaf: The university bought or rented everything in sight to house the post-war enrollment boom.

Inset: Fr. Albert Lemieux, SJ, was Seattle College's last president and Seattle University's first.

social groups began to revive and grow during the 1947/48 school year. Returning veterans swept the student body elections, perhaps because the Veteran's Club held the best dances (in one former student's opinion). The student opera guild staged Gilbert & Sullivan's *Mikado* at the Moore Theatre, but the most attention was reserved for the first post-war Homecoming in January 1948.

With the new year, Father Small could boast that if the post-war enrollment flood was not yet entirely under control, at least it had not swamped the college. Seattle College had grown in more ways than just the number of students. Small now guided an institution with six discrete schools: Arts and Sciences, Nursing, Education, Engineering, Graduate Studies, and Commerce and Finance, and a score of academic departments. Somehow the word "college" seemed too limited for such an institution. Small and his trustees contacted their long-time legal adviser, Charles Moriarty, and began exploring a modest revision in the articles of incorporation.

CAMPION HALL

BOYLSTON HALL

CAROLYN HALL

CAMPBELL HALL

RESIDENCES

FACULTY RESIDENCE

ARTS BLDG

GOFF HALL

HALL

MITCHELL HALL

ENGINEERING BLDG

LOWER CAMPUS

MCHUGH HALL

SEATTLE UNIVERSITY

GYMNASIUM

HALL

VII

LAYING A NEW FOUNDATION

The new corporate documents were unfinished when Father Small received a new assignment in March 1948 to head the Oregon Province. The reins of the college were handed off to Father Edward Flajole, SJ, who had earlier succeeded Small as Dean of the Graduate School, until a permanent successor could be named. That came two months later with the appointment of Father Albert A. Lemieux, SJ.

Only 39 years old, Lemieux was armed with cinematic good looks — Cary Grant comes to mind, but more rugged — and a disarming natural grace which echoed his French Canadian heritage. These were only weapons for a keen organizational mind and the conduits of an inexhaustible reservoir of energy and ideas.

Lemieux was known as "Arby" to his legion of friends, among whom he could count Father Small, a fellow Missoulan and graduate of Loyola High. He was also well acquainted with influential Seattle College faculty members, including Fathers Goodwin, Royce, and Schmid, all of whom had undertaken doctoral studies at the direction of the recently retired provincial, Father Robinson. And he was no stranger to the challenges of administering a Jesuit college, having just finished a tour as dean at Gonzaga under the guidance of Father Corkery.

On May 20, 1948, Lemieux became Seattle College's fifteenth president — and its last. Eight days after his appointment, Lemieux pre-

sided at the commencement ceremonies for 174 graduates, including eight masters of arts and an honorary doctor of laws for the venerable Monsignor Ryan, class of '09. At Lemieux's side on the dais sat Seattle's new Bishop Co-adjutor Thomas Connolly (Bishop Shaughnessy had suffered a stroke).

Father Lemieux took the rostrum on May 28, 1948, and made the following announcement to the dignitaries, graduates, students, faculty, parents and college supporters who filled Memorial Gymnasium:

In view of the great growth that has taken place from a college of liberal arts to an institution now embracing the college of arts and sciences, the schools of commerce and finance, of education, of nursing, of engineering, and of graduate studies, the State [of Washington] has graciously acceded, on this occasion of the golden jubilee of the founding of Seattle College, to the petition of the trustees for the right to the name and charter of Seattle University.

We now proceed as a university and our graduates this evening enjoy the privilege of being its first graduates.

Seattle University still had a way to go before it could live up to its new name, and no one knew the school's limitations better than Lemieux. Among these could be counted a ramshackle physical plant and woefully inadequate student housing. Faculty salaries were seriously below par. There were no endowments or other reliable funding base, and the annual tuition of $180 exceeded the University of Washington's rate but fell short of the cost of educating each student. Finally, the college lacked any active connection to its namesake city outside of a small but loyal Catholic community. In addressing this last deficiency, Lemieux believed, lay the solution to all the rest.

Like Garrand half a century before, Lemieux had an appreciation of ceremony, and he was not going to let the happy accident of the golden jubilee of Seattle College's original charter pass without exploiting its full public relations value. The premiere event was a dinner address on November 16 by Clare Booth Luce, author, activist and wife of the publisher of *Time* and *Life* magazines, who packed the Olympic Hotel's Spanish Ballroom with 500 college supporters. From that time forward, Lemieux made it a point to schedule nationally prominent speakers for commencements and other special events.

The new school year had already begun,

59

Fr. Edward Flajole, SJ, served as interim president in 1948.

Midway during the Chieftains' historic victory over the Harlem Globetrotters, Louis Armstrong presents a trophy to the O'Brien twins, coach Al Brightman and athletic director Bill Fenton. (Courtesy of John and Jeanne O'Brien)

and it also packed the halls back on campus with 2,500 full-time and 400 part-time students. The book store greeted them with a closeout sale on "Seattle College" mugs, book covers and other obsolete novelties. The Jubilee Homecoming the following January brought Governor Arthur Langlie to the Civic Auditorium (since remodeled to become Seattle Center's Opera House) where he bestowed the crown on Queen Elizabeth Ierulli. At commencement that June, 290 graduates heard a valedictory by John Spellman, who would occupy the Governor's Mansion 31 years later.

The college's burgeoning population compelled Lemieux to purchase or rent more houses; the school's motley real estate holdings soon numbered the original Campion and Bellarmine Halls, and Nevin, Caroline, Bordeaux, Mitchell, Goff, McHugh, and Boylston Halls, plus rooms in the Casarucia Apartments and most nearby hotels. To bring order to this chaos, Lemieux began drafting plans for new construction including a decent residence for the Jesuit community, which occupied three dilapidated houses where the Casey Building now stands, a women's dormitory and a new classroom building. His students had different priorities, and they pledged in 1949 to raise $400,000 toward construction of a student union building.

Lemieux knew the university could not yet afford to commit to any major development, so he spent 1949 laying the foundations for his outreach into the greater Seattle community. He established the university's first office of public relations under Father John Kelley, SJ, and contacted leading Catholic women and the wives of current and potential university benefactors with the idea of forming a guild to promote culture in the school's name. Aptly, one of the new Guild's first presentations featured international columnist Dorothy Thompson, the inspiration for Katherine Hepburn's role as *Woman of the Year.* For his part, Lemieux was always careful to acknowledge the generosity of women in building the school.

Enrollment grew steadily until 1950, when the outbreak of the Korean War resulted in a drop of 500, despite the fact that the university was finally organizing its own Reserve Officer Training Corps (ROTC). At the same time, the campus continued to integrate its mostly white student body with other races and cultures.

Dorothy Laigo, her brother Val and her future husband Fred Cordova were among the growing number of Filipino-Americans on campus. Dorothy Cordova remembers that the student community was "small enough to know everybody by face if not name" but some white students could not tolerate closer relations with those of other races. Harassment of interracial couples, for example, broke up a campus jazz band which included Quincy Jones (who returned to campus 40 years later to accept an honorary doctorate).

Jesuits had ways to handle such problems, Dorothy Cordova recalls. When Father James Goodwin, SJ, learned that the Intercollegiate Knights group had blackballed Fred Cordova and

Val Laigo, he helped them organize the inter-racial Alpha Phi Omega service club which ultimately eclipsed the "IKs" in prestige. Fred Cordova and Val Laigo went on to serve the university, respectively as its publicist and as a popular professor of art.

In the fall of 1950, the campus undertook one small but significant project, a shrine to Our Lady of the Rosary (Fatima) dedicated to the memory of Father Peronteau, who had died the previous year. Students formed a "Living Rosary" at this shrine on the southwest corner of the Liberal Arts Building's lawn every May 1st. (In 1991, the generosity of several friends of the university made it possible to install a new statue of the Blessed Virgin Mary in place of the vandalized original.)

Lemieux pressed ahead with two reforms. In the first, he relinquished the title of superior of the Jesuit community to Father Christopher McDonnell, then principal of Seattle Prep. This act freed his time for university administration, and it released him from the canonical six-year limitation on a superior's term. The second and more significant change, something he had been working on for some time, was creation of a lay Board of Regents to advise and assist the president and trustees.

Lemieux introduced the seven original regents to the public on January 24, 1951, beginning with its chairman, Thomas J. Bannan, president of Western Gear Works. The other regents were Henry Broderick, one of Seattle's pioneering real estate developers; Dr. H.T. Buckner, who led the "Fighting 50th" during the previous war and remained a mainstay of the university's pre-med and nursing programs; John W. Maloney, who had become one of the state's most prominent architects since designing the Liberal Arts Building 11 years earlier; Charles P. Moriarty, a former Superior Court Justice and effectively the "family attorney" for the Catholic Church in Washington; Paul Pigott, son of William and president of Pacific Car and Foundry; and Howard

Alpha and Omega: The cover of the 1950-51 Chieftain Press Book features Eddie (#3) and Johnny O'Brien in action and the back cover of the 1952-53 press book features the entire "United Nations" team and staff.

The snow which blankets the shrine honoring Fr. Peronteau was only a memory by May 1, when students traditionally formed a "Living Rosary" in its forecourt.

H. Wright, president of the city's largest general contractors.

Administrative and financial decisions were retained by the university's five Jesuit trustees, but the regents' practical power grew quickly. Part of their charge was to provide "adequate avenues of liaison with the community and state." You could not have assembled a more impressive panel to plug the university into Seattle's business "old boy network." Lemieux's first use of the regents' influence was to win City Council approval of the vacation of 10th Avenue between Madison and Marion — a "gift" of a city street.

A far more audacious exercise of the university's new prestige was an application to the federal government for a $1.2 million loan to build a new women's dormitory, which it received thanks to the sponsorship of Senator Warren G. Magnuson. "Maggie" had been a friend of the college since his days representing central Seattle in the State Legislature, and his intercession produced millions in government grants and loans during a quarter century of Congressional leadership.

Lemieux's next step was to ask George Stuntz, class of '25 and now a leading attorney, to organize Seattle University Associates as a permanent fund raising mechanism in the community. In seeking contributions from the public, Lemieux received a powerful boost from Chieftains coach Al Brightman and twin brothers by the name of John and Ed O'Brien, recruited two years earlier.

Father Carmody, who served as athletic director when not running the English department, had hired Al Brightman in 1948. A former guard for the Boston Celtics and player-manager for the "Seattle Athletics," a regional league basketball team and professional baseball player, Brightman had a keen eye for talent on both the court and the diamond.

Brightman first saw the O'Brien twins in action at a baseball game in Wichita in the spring of 1949. When his friend, Bob Bilgrave, who had played ball in Mt. Vernon and was admissions director at Johns Hopkins, told him about their basketball prowess, he knew he had to have them. Brightman tracked them back to their home in South Amboy, New Jersey. He and the new athletic director, Willard "Bill" Fenton, wrote and lured the brothers to Seattle with partial scholarships.

Expecting a hero's welcome, the O'Briens eagerly enplaned for the long trans-continental flight (a day's travel at the time), but no one greeted them on landing in Seattle-Tacoma Airport early on the morning of October 1, 1949. They took a bus into town and transferred on First Avenue to another bus whose driver "thought" he went by Seattle University. Ed O'Brien remembers thinking, "What have we gotten ourselves into?!" Brightman, it seems, had exaggerated the university's stature in recruiting the O'Briens.

The bus deposited them at the campus, which was only just stirring awake. The brothers entered the Liberal Arts Building, where a tall priest asked if he could be of help. They replied that they were looking for Al Brightman. John O'Brien remembers that the priest's face turned ashen as he looked down on the pair, each of whom stood barely 5 feet, 9 inches tall. "You're not the O'Briens?" he asked warily. "Yes, Father, we are," Ed replied. "Oh my God!" the priest exclaimed and turned on his heel without another word. It turned out that Brightman also had exaggerated the O'Briens' stature in promoting them to Father Lemieux, who had just met his star basketball players.

The O'Briens were superb baseball players and repeatedly led their team into regional NCAA play, but basketball was the game that made them household names. They impressed their new classmates and home town from the beginning by introducing the freshman squad, nicknamed the Papooses, to an entirely new style of game.

"When you're smaller" John O'Brien explains, "pressure offense is the only way to play." The fast break was also the style preferred on the East Coast and unknown to most western players. The O'Briens exploited their almost telepathic simpatico on the court, by which Ed usually set up the goal for John. Being identical twins helped in another way: they often confused referees and took each other's foul calls to stay in the game.

The O'Briens more than fulfilled expectations as varsity players in their first season, racking up 30 wins and only four losses and earning Seattle University its first national ranking. The 1951/52 season "went stratospheric" when the Chieftains stunned the Harlem Globetrotters by a score of 84 to 81 in a Seattle exhibition game on January 21, 1952. This earned the Chieftains a trip the following March to the National Invitational Tournament in Madison Square Garden where the "Gold Dust Twins" impressed national sportswriters even as the Chieftains fell to the Holy Cross Crusaders.

Their second season ended with 29 wins and eight losses, and John became the first college player to score more than 1,000 points in a single season. Thanks to a little help from team publicist Jack Gordon (who later became Seattle's "unofficial greeter" and recently retired as long-time head of the state restaurant association), the "Flyin' O'Briens" and "Johnny O" were soon household names and the subject of stories in *Newsweek* and *Time* magazines. John O'Brien credits Seattle's successes to its "United Nations team" which included Wayne Sanford and Oscar Holden, both African-Americans, Ray Soo, a Chinese-American, and other players of diverse European ancestries.

The O'Briens' next and last season was no less impressive. They beat New York University in Madison Square Garden and the Chieftains earned their first invitation to NCAA tournament play. By the end of the 1952/53 season, John had racked up a college career total of 2,733 points and was named All-American by consensus among all the national polls — Seattle University's first, but not its last.

Lemieux knew that the university had to succeed at more than just basketball, and he did not neglect development of its intellectual resources. One of the first new faculty members to arrive was Father James Royce, a young psychologist recruited by Father McGoldrick.

Chairman Tom Bannan leads a meeting of the Board of Regents in 1956.

Regents such as PACCAR president Paul Pigott and business Dean Paul Volpe gave the university new credibility.

Fr. James Goodwin, SJ, finessed prejudice in one fraternal group by creating a multi-racial competitor.

Filipino students such as Dorothy and Fred Cordova, pictured here in 1991, became life-long university supporters. (Chris Nordfors)

Nazleh Vizetelly and Dorothy Walsh won accreditation for the School of Nursing.

Fr. James Royce, SJ, became an expert on alcoholism in order to counsel students with drinking problems in the early 1950s.

Nick Damascus brought passion and skill to his popular art classes.

As a student, Robert Harmon helped with campus landscaping before becoming a popular history professor.

Now famed as an expert on alcoholism, Royce first encountered the subject tangentially through his work as a pastoral counselor, which brought him into contact with students who had drinking problems. In trying to help them, he naturally turned to the existing psychological literature for guidance, but found there was none. So Royce began scouring records and interviewing the few available experts to assemble an overview of what was then known about the causes and treatment of alcoholism. This, in turn, became the basis of a course launched in 1950, which progressively expanded into a special curriculum (in which he still teaches) and led Royce to compile the first comprehensive college text on the subject, *Alcohol Problems and Alcoholism*, first published in 1981.

For all of this, Royce's first love was the philosophical dimensions of psychology (summarized in his *Man and Meaning*). William Guppy, a young graduate student whom Royce recruited, had exactly the opposite focus, that is, on the clinical dimensions. This made him the perfect candidate to help Royce organize the university's pathfinding Psychological Service Center in 1952, which offered testing, diagnostic evaluations and counseling to students attending the university and Diocesan schools.

Many new faces appeared on the faculty in those years. Among those who would help reshape the university were Nick Damascus, who brought an ardent Greek temperament to his art classes, and Father Frank Wood, SJ, an electrical engineer who soon became captivated by a new kind of machine called a "computer." Other new professors were not strangers to the campus. Returning graduates on the faculty included historian Robert Harmon and sociologists Anita Yourglich and J.R. "Bob" Larson.

Meanwhile, under the leadership of Nazleh Vizetelly, dean from 1944 to 1951, and her successor Dorothy Walsh, the School of Nursing focused its efforts on achieving accreditation. Their work led to approval of the school's public

Marion Hellenkamp became the first African-American elected to student office in 1952.

health program in 1952, followed by full accreditation in 1954.

The 1952/53 school year ended with the opening of the new Chieftain Student Union Building, the first new construction since 1940. Another milestone that school year was the election of Marion Hellenkamp as ASSU secretary, making her the first African-American student body officer. Hellenkamp also edited that year's *Aegis*, which listed among its graduating seniors John and Ed O'Brien.

The O'Briens decided to pursue careers in professional baseball, and Bing Crosby (a graduate of Gonzaga but a Chieftain fan) encouraged them to play for the Pittsburgh Pirates in which he held an interest. They agreed, but neither brother told the other that he had decided to propose marriage to a Seattle University co-ed — on the same day.

By then, Lemieux had presided over a different kind of engagement: that of Seattle University to the larger community. Like any human relationship, this new partnership would be tested by internal conflict and external circumstance, but that lay ahead. First came the honeymoon.

Thousands attended the opening of the Chieftain, including Bishop Connolly and 1925 grads Henry Ivers, Howard LeClair and George Stuntz.

Overleaf: Regents' chairman Tom Bannan and Fr. Lemieux examine a model of the original science building which bears Bannan's name.

Inset: Students plan for a session of the "Model United Nations" on campus.

BUILDING A UNIVERSITY

The Korean War ground to an inconclusive truce during the summer of 1953, and enrollment for the new school year rebounded as a new generation of veterans returned to campus. The Baby Boom was detonating across the nation and Father Lemieux noted that "every college student of 1970 has already been born." Future prospects were bright as far as the eye could see, and if in the past it had seemed that the world was conspiring to make Seattle College fail, events now appeared to guarantee Seattle University's success.

During the post-war boom of the 1950s, what attracted students to a ramshackle campus in the central area? Tuition was far less at the University of Washington and it offered more in aid, facilities and educational options. Despite its special cachet as a Jesuit school and its status as a private university, most of Seattle University's students were children of the working class, studying hard in the hope of gaining entry into the professional middle class. In this quest, Seattle University could offer few scholarships and, as a religious institution, no government financial aid beyond the G.I. Bill. Parents and students worked hard to raise the $500 or so it cost to attend Seattle University for a year, and most classes were deliberately concentrated in the mornings to leave students their afternoons for part-time and often full-time employment.

The secret of Seattle University's appeal boils down to one word — community — in its religious, intellectual and social dimensions.

Seattle University was explicitly, if not exclusively, a Catholic university where the soul received as much attention as the brain and the body. Catholic ritual set the rhythm for life on campus, beginning with the Mass of the Holy Spirit, which inaugurated each academic year, and the Baccalaureate Mass which brought it to a close. In between, mass was being offered every day and night somewhere on campus. In November, all students participated in a mandatory three-day "Retreat." Catholics prayed and attended services and workshops on their faith and non-Catholics were encouraged to meditate and study religious philosophy. Every May 1, many students participated in the Living Rosary at the shrine of the Blessed Virgin Mary, and many volunteered for the numerous groups serving the Archdiocese (which Seattle became in 1951) and its charities. It all added up to a

sense of connectedness which attracted students of many different religious persuasions.

Another attraction lay in the caliber and content of the education, which demanded study and more study under the modified but still exacting strictures of the *Ratio Studiorum* as encapsulated in the Core Curriculum. Regardless of his or her specialization, every student was required to complete the following before graduation:

English — 20 credit hours
Foreign Language — 20
Philosophy — 26
Mathematics and/or Science — 8 to 10
Speech — 5
Theology — 16 (Catholics only)
ROTC — 12 (Men only)

A total of 180 (196 for Catholics) hours was required for a bachelor's degree, and most students completed their "core" in their first two years before switching over to the electives needed to satisfy their majors. They would have to refresh their memories because graduation also required passage of the dreaded Comprehensive Examination. This was essentially a "bar exam" for life, focusing on Scholastic philosophy and theology. The goal, as Father Royce once put it, was to help the student "bring his philosophical views into a unity." The comprehensive began as an oral examination and then shifted to a written test in 1953, as campus growth demanded a less time-consuming procedure. It was aban-

The 1950s were truly happy days at Seattle University as students donned freshman beanies during registration, mugged for the camera during the Sadie Hawkins Day Tolo, and put on their brightest smiles for Homecoming festivities.

doned 10 years later, when, in Royce's words, the exam was resulting in "more students trying to beat the system than trying to study philosophy."

If the large state universities were already becoming "knowledge factories" in the 1950s, Seattle University remained a neighborhood workshop. The faculty in 1955 numbered 38 Jesuits, one Dominican (Father John Fearon), and 64 lay men and women. Then as today, the ratio of students to teachers never exceeded the low double-digits. No "teaching assistants" were employed and professors routinely conducted their own classes, from the most elementary introductions to the most advanced graduate seminars. This fact attracted professors more interested in the give-and-take of the classroom than in garnering research grants or publishing scholarly articles.

The extraordinary degree of student access to their teachers was augmented by the fact that the Jesuits not only worked on campus, they lived there. When not in class, they were available virtually around the clock to tutor, assist or counsel. Their black cassocked figures brought a special dignity to the campus scene, even if their behavior was not always what one expected from intellectual priests.

A typical day might find Father McGoldrick on the mall between classes handing passing students fruit and cookies which he expropriated from the Jesuits' table. There was Father Michael Toulouse, SJ, holding impromptu seminars in the Chieftain, cadging cigarettes and dispensing philosophy. He made a point of reminding his students that "God has a sense of humor, too," and won equal affection from starry-eyed undergraduates and the experienced business leaders who attended his "Executive Thinking" courses.

Another familiar campus figure was Father Hayden Vachon, SJ, rattling his "eke box" to collect spare change to fund a fine arts building (he had raised $70,000 by his death in 1972). The Jesuits also made time for students who needed personal advice or help. Father Louis Sauvain, SJ, earned the nickname "Sam Landers" for his work with young marrieds, and Father Joseph Maguire, SJ, later became a popular chaplain who still serves the alumni.

After the classes were done and the books finally closed for the night, a little time was left over for social life. There were the big events such as Homecoming, Chieftains' games, Valentine's Day "Tolo" Dance, and little events such as luaus and "informals." And there was a club for every interest: The Mendel Club for biologists, the Gavel Club for future lawyers and politicians, engineers' clubs for every specialty, the math club, the commerce club, philosophy club, marketing club, sailing club, and the peripatetic Hiyu Coolees. If academic societies and service groups weren't enough, the most ambitious students could also get involved in campus government through the ASSU or the independent Associated Women Students of Seattle University. Those with any time left to save the world could participate in the Model United Nations or join the active chapters of the Young Democrats or Young Republicans.

Although welcome in all of these clubs, women had their own special groups as well. These included the Alpha Tau Delta nursing

honorary society, the Spurs and Kappa Gamma Pi service groups, Silver Scroll and Gamma Pi Epsilon for honor students, and the "Town Girls" for co-eds outside of the dorms. Male students could join the Intercollegiate Knights, Alpha Phi Omega, and the Alpha Sigma Nu honor student fraternity, among other men-only organizations. These groups specialized in sponsoring some of the dizzier events on campus, such as the annual beard-growing contest, goldfish-swallowing, and tortoise-racing. There were no fraternity or sorority houses as such, and therefore no hazing, but everyone had to endure the collective indignity of wearing "frosh beanies" during his or her first days at the university.

Any student's remaining spare time was absorbed by sports, both on the field and in the bleachers. Al Brightman's Chieftains ended another impressive season in NCAA tournament play featuring a new All-American, Joe Pehanick. The summer of 1955 saw new athletic triumphs for university students as Pat Lesser won the national amateur women's golf championship and Janet Hopps later took the Women's Intercollegiate Tennis championship.

The college students of the 1950s have been dismissed by social critics as the "silent generation," passive, conformist, and devoid of social conscience. At least at Seattle University, the truth is that they were too exhausted after working, studying and playing to change the world beyond campus.

Lemieux was busy as well. In the spring of 1954, he further modernized management of the university by creating the new posts of Academic Vice President and Executive Vice President, to which Fathers James McGuigan, SJ, and John Kelley, SJ, were named respectively. Their number one goal was to transform the rag-tag campus into a modern facility. The first step was construction of a spacious new women's dormitory, Marycrest, at the corner of James and Summit. It was dedicated on October 17, 1954, in ceremonies presided over by Senator Mag-

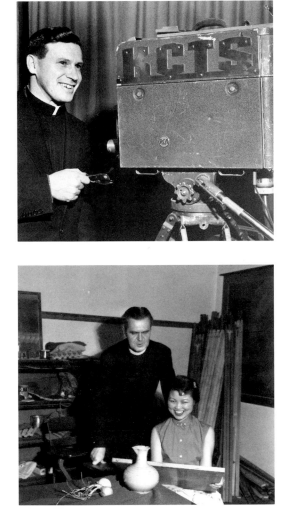

Fr. Michael Toulouse, SJ, (top) was a captivating lecturer and a pioneer in educational television in Seattle. Fr. Haydon Vachon, SJ, collected spare change from students to fund a new home for the fine arts department.

SEATTLE U.'s HALL OF FAME

Pat Lesser and Janet Hopps won the university new distinction on the golf course and tennis court.

Marycrest Hall opened in 1954 as the university's first women's dormitory. It was later sold to Swedish Hospital and demolished.

Editorial art celebrates Seattle University's athletic superstars in the 1950s.

nuson, who had already announced another $1.2 million in federal loans for new construction. This was followed by a men's dormitory, Xavier Hall, which opened in September and was formally dedicated on January 31, 1956 (it later alternated office and residential use). Loyola Hall, the new Jesuit residence (dubbed by Royce as a "home for unwed Fathers") also opened in January and was dedicated the following March.

The new buildings quickly filled as total registration surged past the 3,000 mark in 1956. A Stanford Research Institute study forecast that enrollment could exceed 4,000 and possibly reach 5,000 by the year 1965. Although the study couched this projection, based chiefly on an extrapolation of demographic trends, in exceedingly cautious terms, the enrollment forecast was treated as a virtual fait accompli for planning campus development, and the future of the university and millions of dollars were risked on its accuracy. It turned out to be an imprudent calculation, but at the moment there seemed to be no limits to the university's potential growth.

The university struggled to keep up with its own expansion. In 1956, the Ford Foundation awarded the university $432,900 for the express purpose of upgrading its faculty salaries, which still lagged far behind those for comparable schools. The City turned additional streets over to Lemieux to consolidate his campus. He purchased the nearby Langendorf Bakery, Anderson

& Thompson Building, and later, the venerable Casarucia Apartments on Marion Street. This was renamed "Marian Hall" in 1960 which caused no end of spelling confusion.

Where was the money coming from for all of this development? Seattle restaurateur Victor Rosellini was one benefactor recruited by the university. Rosellini remembers with a laugh that Lemieux's development director, Father Gerard Evoy, SJ, "hoodwinked" him into more than one unplanned gift. "All priests have a way of getting what they want if they think you can give it," Rosellini warns, adding, "I never met a Jesuit I didn't like."

On October 1, 1956, ground was broken for the new home for the Schools of Commerce and Finance and Education. At that ceremony, Lemieux revealed that regent Paul Pigott had pledged $500,000 to the university, in appreciation for which the new building would now be dedicated to his father, William Pigott. That same October, Lemieux announced the expansion of the Board of Regents to eleven and named its first woman member, Mrs. Albert Schafer, a leading philanthropist. Three more business leaders joined, headed up by William E. Boeing, Jr., son of the airplane giant's founder and president of Mesabi-Western Corporation. At the same time, the Boeing Airplane Company (in which the Boeing family no longer played a role) leased the basement of Xavier for a special on-campus design support group involving university students.

Lemieux also made some significant changes in staffing during the 1956/57 academic year. He named Father Evoy to the new post of vice president for development, elevated Father John "Jack" Fitterer, SJ, to dean of arts and sciences, and placed the Psychological Service Center in the capable hands of Father Louis Gaffney, SJ. Previously, Sister Mary Ruth Niehoff, OP, had succeeded Ruth Walsh as dean of the School of Nursing in 1954, and Al Brightman had departed due to illness. The new athletic director, Vince

Sister Mary Ruth Niehoff, OP, (far left) was an effective and popular dean of nursing. William Boeing, Jr., joined the Regents in 1956 and helped to guide the university for two decades. Mrs. Albert Schafer became the first woman to serve on the Board of Regents in 1956.

Cazzetta, and John Castellani, an assistant coach from Notre Dame, took charge of the Chieftains.

Castellani had a new star on his hands. Elgin Baylor had been recruited from the College of Idaho at Caldwell in 1955, but NCAA rules prevented him from playing as a Chieftain for one year. He stayed in shape with the help of Claude Norris, the university's long-time trainer (one of the few African-Americans then serving in the Seattle Police Department) and John O'Brien, who coached him on Westside Ford's semi-pro team. When he finally got to play, "The Rabbit," as Baylor had been nicknamed by his uncle, was soon breaking Johnny O's old records. By the end of the 1957 season, he had led the Chieftains to fifth place in the national rankings.

While his Chieftains earned fame on the basketball court, Father Lemieux achieved the distinction of being named "First Citizen" for 1956 by the Seattle Real Estate Board. The award was nothing less than the seal of approval by the city's economic establishment, something Lemieux had set out to obtain for the university nine years earlier. Governor Albert Rosellini presided over a 1957 Homecoming celebration whose "Vapor Trails" theme was inspired by Boeing's new 707 jet liners, and Boeing president William Allen gave the commencement address.

The following fall, the new Pigott Building opened its doors to help accommodate more than 3,400 students. It was the first new classroom building since 1941. October 1957 provided a boost from an unlikely source when the Soviet Union launched the first artificial Earth satellite. The nation was shocked and embarrassed by this triumph of communist technology, and Lemieux was quick to draw the moral, "Perhaps in this age of Sputnik, the wisdom of investing in education can be presented more forcefully." Lemieux made sure that Seattle University would reap its fair share of the educational largess generated by the "space race."

As Father Lemieux celebrated his 10th year as president in 1958, the Chieftains seemed on their way to deliver a unique anniversary present, the NCAA championship. On March 21, Baylor led his team into the semi-finals in Lexington, Kentucky, where they crushed number-one ranked Kansas State 73 to 51. But it was a costly victory in which Baylor was injured, something which the University of Kentucky exploited in the following night's championship game. All but sidelined in brutally physical play, Baylor watched an early lead evaporate as his team went down 72 points to Kentucky's 84.

It was a disappointment, but second place was still not bad for a little Jesuit school way out in Seattle. Father Lemieux led 6,000 fans to the airport to greet the returning team. They cheered, but some sports writers and other NCAA

Coach John Castellani and publicist Jack Gordon flank the 1956-57 Chieftains which included a new star, Elgin Baylor, wearing number 22.

Baylor powers the Chieftains toward their fateful rendezvous with the University of Kentucky in the 1958 NCAA "Final Four."

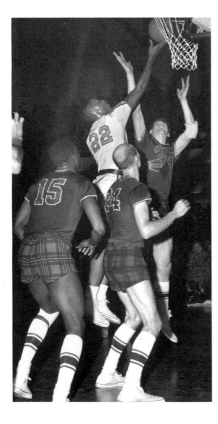

coaches didn't join in. They smelled a rat on this "Cinderella Team." The story broke in April that coach Castellani had extended sundry privileges to players during recruitment and training, a little cash here, a free trip there. The violations were penny-ante and routine at most schools, but they provided more than enough for envious NCAA coaches to sideline Baylor, who was eligible to play one more season. The officials voted to suspend Seattle University from NCAA play for two years. Castellani resigned with the bitter-sweet observation, "I feel that about everything that could happen to a coach has happened here."

The campus was stunned, but it could take some consolation in the pro-ball success of Baylor, who quickly turned around the moribund Minneapolis Lakers. He went on to earn universal praise as one of the best all-round players in the sport, and Baylor is now general manager of the Los Angeles Clippers. The job of putting Seattle University's team back together fell to another Chieftain star, Ed O'Brien, who replaced Vince Cazzetta as athletic director when Cazzetta took over coaching the varsity squad. The team would recover and produce more great stars such as "Sweet" Charlie Brown, Eddie Miles and Tom Workman, but it would

never again reach the heights achieved in 1958—
and the athletics department had not heard its
last of scandal.

Not one to dwell on disappointment, Lemieux forged ahead with new plans during 1958.
These included organizing the faculty for a new
college for nuns called "Sister Formation" being
developed by the Sisters of Providence under
the guidance of Sister Mary Philothea. A later
member of the faculty, Sister Rosaleen Trainor,
CSJP, praised this program as "a significant
movement to educate women for leadership, to
break out of the 'Yes, Father' mode." Early
hopes that this college would be located at Seattle University were dashed when the Sisters
decided to develop their own campus at Providence Heights at a cost of $6 million.

The deepening relationship between the
Boeing Company and the university reached a
new level that year when the former sponsored
a master's program in electrical and mechanical
engineering. This promptly enrolled 125, all but
eight of whom were Boeing employees. Also in
1958, the National Science Foundation awarded
a $68,000 grant for the college to train high
school science teachers during the coming summer, and Lemieux launched a $2,150,000 fund
drive for a new science building.

In April 1959, a new fountain was installed
north of Pigott as a sanctuary and memorial to
Mary Broderick, wife of regent Henry Broderick. Also that month, Father Lemieux received the unique honor of being named Man of
the Year by the Seattle lodge of the B'nai B'rith.
Victor Rosellini, for one, had urged the university to reach out to the Jewish community. Irving
Anches joined the Board of Regents, and SU
later took the unprecedented step of inviting an
Orthodox Rabbi, Arthur Jacobovitz, to lecture
on Judaism. In June 1959, actress-turned-diplo-
mat Irene Dunne became the first woman to
deliver the university's commencement address.
Monsignor Ryan presided over the granting of
367 degrees. It would be the last such cere-

*Fr. Lemieux dedicates
the Chief Seattle
fountain to the memory
of Regent Henry
Broderick's wife, Mary.*

*On behalf of B'nai
B'rith Lodge 503, Rabbi
Raphael Levine honors
Fr. Lemieux for fostering
religious and racial
understanding.*

mony for the 1909 graduate, who died January 23, 1960.

The 1950s had been a dramatic and formative decade in Seattle University's development. Seattle University, like most of America, looked forward to the 1960s as another decade of assured progress. Things did not work out quite according to plan.

Campaign fever gripped the campus in 1960 thanks to the entry of the first serious Catholic contender for U.S. president since Al Smith. Curiously, Seattle University students were slow to warm to Senator John Kennedy, and a straw poll favored Adlai Stevenson for the Democratic nomination. This quickly turned around when Ted Kennedy visited the campus a few weeks before the election and packed Pigott Auditorium with 400 cheering supporters for his brother.

Lemieux undertook another reorganization. He consolidated the functions of publicity, alumni services, and fund raising under a new vice presidency for University Relations, to which Father Evoy was named. He also won approval to enlarge the Board of Regents to 16 members. The

new decade began on a sad note with the sudden death of Paul Pigott on January 23, 1961. As he would have wanted, campus development continued with work on a new Bellarmine Hall. The Science Building, named for Thomas Bannan, was completed in time for the new school year and the Sister Formation College also opened in a spectacular new campus at Providence Heights.

Seattle's "Century 21" world's fair, on whose board Lemieux served, fueled more optimism during 1962. A 10-year university development plan was adopted, and students assessed themselves a special fee to raise $800,000 for a new library. This must have heartened veteran librarian Father Vincent Conway, SJ, who had begged and borrowed for years to build his collection housed in the Administration Building. He knew more than anyone else that the existing library was woefully inadequate in both space and content. Correcting these deficiencies would have to wait for Congress to pass crucial legislation needed to fund the $2.8 million facility.

In February 1963, a new sport scandal rock-

ed the campus when coach Cazzetta angrily resigned, castigating athletic director Ed O'Brien for interfering with the team. Lemieux defended O'Brien in an open letter which said that Cazzetta had demanded too much power. O'Brien named Clair Markey to fill in for Cazzetta until Bob Boyd became the permanent coach.

That settled, May 1963 gave Seattle University a fresh sense of triumph as alumnus Jim Whittaker became the first American to conquer Mount Everest. The university attained a summit of its own when it received federal approval of a $3.8 million loan, its largest yet, for the future Campion Hall. Also that year, the college acquired the former Canada Dry bottling plant on 12th Avenue and began planning a new book store for the site (plans for a new building were later shelved in favor of remodeling the former factory).

The university awarded almost 500 degrees in June 1963. The next month, the Teatro Inigo (honoring Ignatius by using his name in its original Spanish) opened in a former Jehovah's Witness Kingdom Hall at Columbia and Broadway.

Purchased the year before under the prodding of Fr. James Connors, SJ, the new playhouse could be configured for theater-in-the-round, thrust stage or a traditional proscenium. William Dore presented Jean Anouilh's *Ring Around the Moon*, the first of scores of productions he would direct before becoming head of the fine arts department.

In the fall the university took "a giant stride across the threshold of the education of tomorrow," according to campus literature, when it opened its new Computer Center. This represented the culmination of efforts begun in 1957 when Fathers Frank Wood, Louis Gaffney and Paul Luger attended night classes in computing taught by Boeing Company staff on campus. Unfortunately, the nearest computer was located at the University of Washington; six years elapsed before Wood and Gaffney obtained a National Science Foundation grant for Seattle University's own equipment.

Organized under the leadership of Father James Cowgill, SJ, and directed by George Town, the new Computer Center served teaching, research and university business needs with an IBM 1620 system. This machine, although primitive by today's standards, helped put the university in the vanguard of computer science and its educational applications.

The year 1963 had witnessed great progress — and great sadness beginning with the death of Pope John XXIII on June 3 after a papacy of only five years. His humanism and spirit of reform, expressed in *Pacem in terris* and the Second Vatican Council, had reinvigorated Catholic faith and thought, particularly among the young. Then came the assassination of President Kennedy on November 22. Grieving students and faculty filled the gymnasium for a memorial mass within an hour of the President's death. Young Catholics had lost another hero, and more than a little of their innocence.

The examples of President Kennedy and Pope John XXIII and the on-going struggle for civil rights led by Dr. Martin Luther King, Jr.

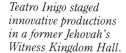

Teatro Inigo staged innovative productions in a former Jehovah's Witness Kingdom Hall.

Dr. M.M. Davies oversees the work of the Peter Claver Tutorial Program staffed by hundreds of student volunteers.

The university hoped to use federal Urban Renewal funds to expand and modernize its campus (see facing page) and construct a space-age gym, but neighbors feared such ambitions might cost them their homes.

Regents' chairman Tom Bannan poses with his successor Bob O'Brien as construction begins on the Lemieux Library.

Shortly before his death, Pope John XXIII honored university Regents with this medal. Fr. Lemieux bids farewell to students in 1965, not knowing that he would return in only a few years.

found special resonance in the social idealism at the core of Jesuit teaching. As a result, more and more students chose to make a personal commitment. For example, Sam Sperry, now Editorial Page Enterprise Editor for the *Seattle Post-Intelligencer*, went to work in Ethiopia under the aegis of Crossroads Africa. This people-to-people aid program was later emulated by the Peace Corps, which attracted a higher percentage of applications at Seattle University than on any other campus.

Other students put their lessons and ideals to work closer to home. The new VISTA program attracted many volunteers such as Winnie Wynhausen (an alumna, and like her husband, Sam Sperry, later an adjunct professor) to help America's poor. Seattle University became a major contributor to the Jesuit Volunteer Corps, and a sizable contingent of students joined Church leaders in campaigning for passage

of Seattle's open housing referendum in the spring of 1964. Voting for the proposed ordinance barring racial discrimination in housing was described as nothing less than a "moral duty" by one priest. Such lofty sentiments did not prevail in a bitterly divisive campaign, and open housing went down by a two-to-one margin in March (federal and state law later accomplished what Seattle voters refused to do).

This experience brought the issue of racism home to a campus surrounded by a declining, largely African-American neighborhood. Bob Larson introduced a course on "Race Relations" in the sociology department. More than 50 students later turned their words into deeds by volunteering to tutor inner city children at the Peter Claver Center, founded after World War II by the Sisters of Providence and Immaculate Conception Parish. This early effort expanded into the Caritas Program (taken from the Latin to express service through love) and sponsored

a variety of literacy and social service programs in Seattle's Central Area.

The university had much to be proud of as a leader for racial justice. As early as 1953, when such commitments were not routine, Father Lemieux put the university on record as "vigorously opposed to all forms of racism or any other 'ism' which denies the basic dignity common to all." Until the Seattle Central Community College was organized in the mid-1960s, the university maintained the highest minority enrollment in the state, higher in both percentage and absolute number than the far larger University of Washington. Seattle University nurtured such notable American and foreign-born minority students as Dr. Noel Brown, a champion debater and honors student who took his bachelor's degree in 1958 and now directs the United Nations' Environmental Program.

But the 1960s elevated standards for equal opportunity, and the contrast between the relatively affluent campus and its impoverished, mostly minority neighbors in the Central Area began to give rise to tensions. These were exacerbated by the university's plan to use federal Urban Renewal funds to expand the campus through the demolition of surrounding homes. The perceived contradictions between the university's stated social idealism and actual practice would soon erupt into political conflict.

Activism was in the air and every topic inspired debate. In 1964, the *Journeyman* supplement in the *Spectator* featured a spirited attack on "Thomistic Dogma" by several students, which elicited heated rebuttals from other students and faculty. At that moment other Catholic campuses were being rocked by controversies involving administration censorship of student newspapers, and Gonzaga experienced student unrest over its housing policies. The Free Speech Movement at Berkeley, which marked the official birth of the student movement, was still months away, but the shape of things to come was emerging.

Seattle University officials were less concerned with growing student activism than with a shrinking enrollment. Father Lemieux had described the fall of 1964 as "the moment of truth in which the predictions of the past will be realized," but not only did enrollment fail to increase, it decreased for the first time in five years. Concerned officials ascribed the drop to the raising of the annual tuition to $645 and they hoped registration would recover once families and students adjusted to the new cost schedule.

No one seems to have asked aloud if something more fundamental was going wrong at the university. Any private misgivings were dispelled when President Lyndon Johnson signed the legislation containing the loan for the long-delayed library. This was followed soon after by the settlement of the probate of Mrs. Loretta Emard's estate, which donated $1 million to the university in return for the pleasure the Chieftains had given her and her husband Henry. Only the deaths

of two old university friends, long-time physics professor Harry Kinerk and the first woman regent, Mrs. Schafer, momentarily darkened the mood on campus that fall.

Lemieux began the 1964/65 school year by unveiling "The Seattle Plan," a sweeping reform of the university's core curriculum begun under Father Ernest Bertin, SJ, and completed by Father Fitterer. Crafted by the university's best minds, the new curriculum attempted to preserve an 80 credit-hour liberal arts core "to instill the habit of wisdom," while adding more flexibility for electives and specialization. It also cut the average course from five to four credit hours, which would prove to be a financial time bomb.

Adoption of the new core turned out to be Lemieux's last major act as president. Ready for a change, Lemieux had the opportunity to participate in the Jesuit congregation which would elect a new Superior General. On February 3, 1965, the new chairman of the regents, PACCAR president Robert O'Brien, announced Lemieux's resignation and selection of Father Jack Fitterer as his successor. Father Lemieux did not escape without one more sports scandal, when three Chieftain stars were implicated in a bribery scandal involving a Chicago gambler. Although the charges were ultimately dropped, the damage was great enough to prompt *Sports Illustrated* to blast the Chieftains, and even the *Spectator* editorialized, "Now is the time to take a long hard look at basketball."

That could wait, however, because the first business was honoring Lemieux for his 17 years of extraordinary service to the university. Praise poured in from around the world, but nothing may have gratified Lemieux more than the ground breaking on April 6 for the new library which would bear his name. After all, Father Lemieux was foremost a builder.

Workmen finish the double-helix stairs of the Lemieux Library, a fitting monument to the university's 15th president.

Overleaf: Students mark the October 15, 1969, "Vietnam Moratorium" on the steps of the Lemieux Library.

Inset: Fr. Jack Fitterer, SJ, took over the driver's seat as Lemieux's successor, but the road ahead would not prove to be smooth.

WARNING SIGNS

*F*ather Jack Fitterer became president on April 8, 1965. He told a *Spectator* reporter that his succession was "like stepping out of a cold shower and into Niagara Falls." For all of that, he "hoped to be the second president to leave office without ulcers." He would not get his wish.

An Ellensburg native and Gonzaga graduate who took his master's degree at St. Louis and attended the Gregorian University in Rome, Father Fitterer was photogenic, articulate and politically adept. He made an excellent impression in the community as a "modern" Jesuit and a natural successor to Lemieux. Unlike Lemieux, Fitterer failed to earn the respect of the faculty, some of whom dismissed him as "Smiling Jack."

Fitterer had cause to smile in the beginning. He had climbed into the driver's seat of what seemed to be a perfectly tuned vehicle with a smooth and straight road stretching ahead. In an interview, he predicted, "By 1985, we will be the Catholic Stanford, or perhaps I should have said, the Catholic Brandeis."

On his first day as president, Fitterer was confronted with a minor campus contretemps. The *Spectator* criticized the use of an ASSU credit card by student body president Mick McHugh (grandson of T.C. McHugh) and ASSU treasurer Kip Toner, who would later become the university's business manager. Fitterer defended the two student officers, who had violated no procedures, but he went further to suppress additional newspaper reports. This permanently soured relations between the *Spectator* and his administration. It was a tempest in a teacup, but not a good omen for Fitterer's prospects in dealing with an increasingly restless and assertive student population.

The incident was quickly eclipsed by news of the accreditation of the School of Business. Fitterer completed plans to demolish the ancient "temporary" buildings purchased after World War II during the summer (Buhr Hall was saved by a last minute reprieve) and to develop a grand new gymnasium on the site of Catholic Memorial Field at 14th and East Cherry. Enrollment recovered to set a new record at almost 4,200 in the fall of 1965, on the low side of previous forecasts but comforting. The university's newest and grandest residence hall, Campion, was nearing completion and the city government vacated the final streets blocking unification of the campus.

That October witnessed a display of pomp and circumstance that would have made Garrand blush as the university installed its sixteenth president and celebrated the golden jubilee of two of its "Four Horsemen of Loyola," Fathers Reidy and Nichols. More festivities followed when Superior General Pedro Arrupe, SJ, visited the campus on April 14, 1966. Selected the year before by an international congregation which included Father Lemieux, Arrupe was the first head of the Society of Jesus to sct foot on American soil.

In a speech to the faculty and students, Arrupe made what would prove to be a particularly trenchant observation, "The Catholic university will fulfill its mission only if there is rapport and understanding and mutual trust between the religious-educator and the lay men and women who share his teaching apostolate."

Fitterer used the balance of the school year to assemble his administrative team. Father Robert Bradley, SJ, had already moved up from the history department to become dean of arts and sciences, and Father Royce was named his assistant. Fathers Frank Costello, Edmund Morton, and Joseph Perri, SJ, respectively became executive, academic and university relations vice presidents. Father McNulty was named head of development, Father Gaffney took over the graduate school, and Father Arthur Earl, SJ, succeeded Dr. Volpe as acting dean of the business school. That summer a department of fine arts was created under the leadership of

Val Laigo finishes his dramatic mural for the library.

Superior General Pedro Arrupe, SJ, visited campus during the first American tour by a head of the Society of Jesus.

school new fame on the tennis court, and Val Laigo finished his colorful murals in time for the dedication of the long-delayed Lemieux Library on April 21, 1967. The following month, Fitterer took an unprecedented step and named the first layman to a vice presidency, William Adkisson for finance. He was joined soon after by Elliott Paulson, as vice president for resource development. These were significant reforms, but they did not address the college's fundamental problems.

Much of the university's financial management woes derived from the new core curriculum, which Fitterer had once called a "portent of the future." He was right. Because the total number of credit hours needed for graduation had not been reduced, the deflation of course credits from five to four demanded a corresponding inflation of instruction time and staff. This combined with declining enrollments to force the university into borrowing against future tuition to pay current costs. Institutions with deep endowments or state subsidies might be able to sustain such deficit spending, but Seattle University had neither. It lived from hand to mouth, year to year, and it could not long survive an operational debt which quickly mounted to $1 million. This shortfall was compounded by the virtual absence of systems to monitor costs and control budgets. As one veteran faculty member recalls those days, "No one was minding the store."

The university's own success in securing federal loans for construction added a further burden as income shrank and operating costs rose. Without an on-going program of fund raising, tuition was the only source of funds for paying the interest on government loans for Marycrest, Xavier, Loyola, Bellarmine and Campion Halls and the Lemieux Library — and balloon payments on their principals were due within a few years. Yet, amazingly in retrospect, Fitterer pressed ahead with plans for a costly new physical education complex on the site of the

Seattle University alumnus and Harvard-trained composer Joseph Gallucci, fulfilling an old dream of Fathers Reidy (who died the following year) and Vachon.

Also that summer, Fitterer completed work on a new plan to raise $5 million for a "Decade of Distinction." Decade of extinction might have been more accurate. When the university hiked tuition 40 percent to $320 a quarter, enrollment promptly plummeted by over 500 students. In Fitterer's defense, tuition was a double-edged sword: raising it cut enrollment; failing to raise it cut income needed to maintain and improve academic quality. Fitterer was only trying to catch up with the university's financial needs, which had suffered from Lemieux's refusal to raise tuition in step with costs. The impact of the higher tuition was compounded by the opening of Seattle Central Community College, which offered a low-cost alternative to Seattle University only a few blocks away. This did not prevent Fitterer from announcing another tuition hike, to $350 per quarter, barely a month into the 1966/67 school year.

Worsening enrollment reports were offset by good news from other departments. Tom Gorman and Steve Hopps were earning the former Catholic Memorial Stadium. The new facility, to be named in honor of Archbishop Connolly, required yet another federal loan and major infusions of community funds that could have been used to pay off older debts or meet operational costs. Meanwhile, the university refused to admit that it was experiencing anything more than a little "financial strain."

Fitterer did not need more trouble but he got it anyway. In November 1967, he directed his assistant, Father Timothy Cronin, SJ, to prevent the *Spectator* from publishing an article written by Dr. Ronald Rousseve. A popular professor of education, Rousseve was one of only two African-American members of the faculty. The title of his censored article was "In Defense of Responsible Permissiveness Toward Sex in the Human Adventure."

Rousseve had raised eyebrows the year before with a *Spectator* piece advocating "humanistic experiential existentialism" in place of Scholastic verities. This and some of Rousseve's classroom pronouncements earned him a "fair warning" letter dated October 20, 1967. The administration cautioned Rousseve that his views "contradict explicit principles of Catholic faith and morals," in violation of his employment contract. Undeterred, Rousseve now proposed to challenge Catholic doctrine on premarital intercourse and birth control in the *Spectator*, which the administration regarded to be a voice of the entire university, not just students. Whether or not officially sanctioned, publication of such views on a Jesuit campus was going too far in the administration's view — and it was especially unwelcome as the university pleaded for support from wealthy, often conservative benefactors.

Reports that the *Spectator* had been censored alarmed many on campus. Even those who did not share Rousseve's views thought the administration had overreacted. The Faculty Senate, formed the year before under the pres-

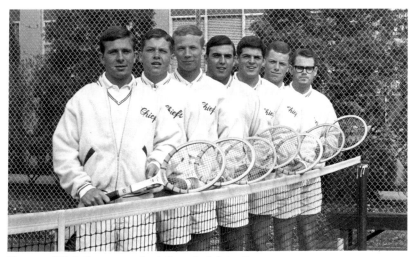

Tennis stars Steve Hopps (first in line) and Tom Gorman (fifth from the front) garnered fresh acclaim for the university.

idency of Bob Larson, asked the administration to reconsider; Fitterer's response was that the Senate "must not get the idea they are a second board of trustees." Students came to Rousseve's defense at a rally sponsored by the Political Union, a bi-partisan group founded in 1963, while the new branch of the American Association of University Professors (AAUP) demanded an investigation.

Fitterer would not relent and it fell to Father Morton to try to negotiate "an amicable solution." He reported to the trustees on January 2, 1968, that "after a somewhat stormy session, Dr. Rousseve agreed to resign." This took effect on March 29, two days after Ruth Watson, director of Advanced Placement and sole remaining African-American on the faculty, tendered her own resignation for career reasons. One week later, Martin Luther King, Jr. was assassinated. Some began to look at Rousseve's treatment from a racial perspective, although Rousseve denied that the dispute involved anything more than academic freedom.

In May, 10 professors of English — two-thirds of that faculty — resigned en masse, blaming "a crisis of confidence in the administration." One, Dr. David Downes, went further and denounced the Jesuits for maintaining a

Fr. Timothy Cronin, SJ, was directed to censor Dr. Ronald Rousseve's controversial views on birth control.

Joseph Gallucci, a composer trained at both Seattle and Harvard Universities, headed the first formal fine arts department.

Dr. James Robertson's revelations about the university's finances shocked the campus and community.

Dr. J. Robert Larson launched the university's first course in inter-racial relations.

Charles Mitchell organized the university's first office for minority students while Brian Cullerton led its institute for urban affairs.

"pastoral ghetto." The Rousseve incident, he said, "really scared us" because the administration's "reaction was irrational and violently conservative." Father Morton tried to downplay the resignations, telling *The Seattle Times*, "This is a normal turnover which should be considered a sign of academic health." Morton was accurate to the degree that the university's worsening financial condition was beginning to be felt by the faculty in higher classloads and deferred raises. Thus, some resignations probably involved economics more than civil liberties, but they were far from healthy. Fitterer had squandered the "rapport and understanding" between Jesuits and lay faculty that Father Arrupe had rightly noted was crucial to a Catholic university's survival.

That same May, a Black Student Union (BSU) was organized by Paul Chiles, the son of Ruth Watson, who explained that he was tired of being the target of racial epithets on the campus. The *Spectator* also denounced "unofficial middle-class bigots" who harassed inter-racial couples. The university's record in promoting racial equality fell under scrutiny in its new *SU Magazine* for alumni. In the inaugural edition, Lawrence Sanford, former Chieftain star and head of the Urban League, acknowledged the work of the 500-plus students who now volunteered for Caritas programs in the Central Area, but he added, "Even SU is an institution which lacks 'color' in areas other than athletics, despite its obvious proximity to the ghetto."

Father William LeRoux, SJ, professor of theology, echoed the challenge: "That we have a prejudice is natural; that we do something to root it out of our minds and hearts is a sign of our Christian maturity." Business dean Dr. James Robertson led a faculty seminar that fall to define an agenda for stronger affirmative action and urban outreach. At this point, there were fewer than 100 African-Americans among 3,500 students, and none remained on the faculty.

During the summer of 1968, Fitterer and his trustees turned their attention to the university's worsening finances. The sales of Bordeaux and McHugh Halls yielded over $125,000, but this was far short of the million-dollar operating deficit projected for fiscal year 1969 (ending June 30, 1969). The trustees thought they had found a savior when they made contact with B.C Ziegler & Company, a major capital underwriter for private schools. Between May and August, the trustees consolidated their existing bank debt and projected deficit into a package of direct obligation serial notes worth $2 million. As collateral, the university pledged its future tuition income and title to the Liberal Arts, Bannan, Engineering and Chieftain Buildings — the university's last unencumbered assets. Although these notes were sold to the Marine National Exchange Bank, the obligation would always be called the "Ziegler debt," and it soon proved to be anything but a salvation.

Enrollment slipped again in the new school year, and on-campus residents fell to 1,076, not even enough to fill Campion Hall. Due to declining tuition and board income, Fitterer soon found himself forced to seek new bank loans to pay faculty and campus bills, piling new debt onto old. In the fall of 1968, the university welcomed Father Lemieux back as Fitterer's special assistant for development. Lemieux's return had nothing to do with Seattle University's deteriorating situation — he had simply wearied of his duties as rector of Spokane's Mount St. Michael Seminary — but the timing could not have been better. Lemieux's first step was to recruit two business powerhouses for the Board of Regents: Eddie Carlson, president of Western Hotels and United Airlines, and Harold Heath, founder of the Heath-Techna Corporation.

Racial issues continued to challenge the university as the 1968 school year opened. Local Black Panther leader Aaron Dixon spoke on campus, and a new Black History course was introduced — but with a white professor, Dr.

Robert Saltvig (later history chairman). He was replaced the following February with Clayton Pitre at the behest of the BSU. Meanwhile, African-American students staged an "Experience Black" dance and later held a separate Homecoming.

Fitterer honored the university's earlier commitments to promote racial justice. A new Urban Affairs Institute was launched under the direction of Brian Cullerton in January 1969 and Jim LaCour, a former Chieftain star, was hired to coordinate Central Area use of the Connolly Center, which was nearing completion. In September 1969, the promised Office of Minority Affairs was created and Charles Mitchell, now president of Seattle Central Community College, took its helm.

Progress was made in other areas as master's programs were introduced in business administration, engineering, teaching and adult education administration. The "Seattle University Masters of Religious Education," or SUMORE program, was also organized. Fitterer had also opened debate, at least with trustees, on issues touching the university's organic character: the growing "separation of the Jesuit community from the university," a new charter of student rights, and the installation of lay members on the board of trustees as Gonzaga had done. Looked at from some distance, the university had already made major reforms in a remarkably brief time, and further trouble might have been averted despite the superheated expectations of the 1960s. But other forces were closing in.

Declining enrollment and rising costs forced Fitterer to close Marycrest Hall and put it on the market. Women students were transferred to the half-empty Campion. What many referred to as the "Jesuit Folly on James" became in February 1969 the first co-ed dorm at a Jesuit college. Two months later, the Sisters of Providence faced their own set of realities and closed their $6 million campus at Providence Heights.

The reforms of the Second Vatican Council and limited funds spelled the end of the Sister Formation College at Providence Heights in 1969.

Campion Hall was derided as a "Jesuit Folly" even during construction in 1965. Students supported Dr. Patricia Smith's medical mission in Vietnam but their views on America's military mission eventually soured.

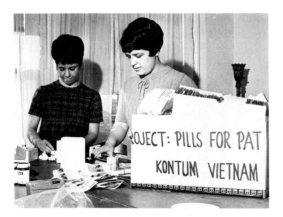

The Sister Formation Program had become a victim of the post-Vatican II climate which favored involvement over seclusion.

The war in Vietnam was becoming an issue. Seattle University students were not ignorant of nor indifferent to Vietnam; as early as 1954, an editor of the *Spectator* had warned, "The possibility of active American participation in Indo-China should not be surprising." Students and faculty had long supported university graduate Dr. Patricia Smith in bringing medical services to the Montagnards in central Vietnam. Her clinic was overrun by the Viet Cong in March 1968; Dr. Smith barely escaped. Such involvement helps to explain why SU students were late to abandon their support of the American war effort. Yet, when Senator Robert Kennedy had visited the campus in October 1966, almost the entire student body packed the gym to hear him question Lyndon Johnson's policies, albeit gently at that time.

Most Seattle University students were still accustomed to trusting presidents and parents, which prompted Edward Keating, then editor of the left-wing Catholic magazine *Ramparts* to comment, "This is the first campus I've visited where the students are more conservative than the faculty." On January 24, 1968, amid the Tet Offensive, the *Spectator* reported a survey in which students supported American involvement two-to-one. On May 10, a new survey showed that the ratio had flipped, a month before Senator Kennedy's assassination shocked the campus.

By October 1968, the opponents of the war and members of the New Left organized the Student Involvement League and staged a teach-in against the war. The following February, a freshman and Gonzaga honor student (unaffiliated with SIL) set fire to the ROTC hall which stood opposite Loyola. Damage was minor but the significance was great: the war had arrived on the university's doorstep. When Archbishop Connolly endorsed bombing Hanoi, many stu-

dents and not a few members of the faculty walked out of the June 1969 commencement.

Fitterer struggled to keep the university under control. On the positive side, he faced the problems created by his own "Seattle Plan" and tapped chemistry professor Gary Zimmerman to chair a review of the Core Curriculum. He also pressed ahead with discussions which would lead to the addition of lay members to the board of trustees. The decline of enrollment slowed due to the success of the new MBA and SU-MORE programs in attracting new graduate students.

By this time the Ziegler loan had been spent. Fitterer continued to borrow to meet a $531,000 operating deficit in fiscal year (FY) 1969 and a shortfall of $919,000 forecast for FY 1970. This did not deter the university from pursuing a $1.3 million loan from the federal department of Health, Education and Welfare (HEW) for construction of Connolly Center.

Just as plans were announced for student demonstrations in connection with the nationwide Vietnam Moratorium on October 15, 1969, Fitterer picked up his censor's pen one more time. He halted printing of *SU Magazine* and forced deletion of two articles written by Roger Yockey, a campus writer who later became a labor organizer, and Dr. Robertson, whom Fitterer had replaced with Gerald Cleveland as business dean. The magazine's topic was the issue of dissent, and Robertson had plenty to say.

Robertson's proposal to separate the business school financially from the rest of the university had been rebuffed by Fitterer, and there was no love lost between the two men. Robertson and Yockey's censored views found an immediate outlet in the *Spectator*, where Robertson revealed the university's dire financial straits in full detail. He warned that if dramatic changes were not made soon, the university "will have to sell out to the state," and he ripped Fitterer's

administration for "killing imagination and initiative and ultimately the institution itself."

The entire university community was stunned. This latest act of censorship moved one-third of the student body to sign a petition demanding a new "bill of rights" on campus, and tensions helped to turn the Vietnam Moratorium into the first sizable anti-war demonstration on campus. Fearing disruptions, the administration cancelled classes and the Mass of the Holy Spirit. To both liberals and conservatives, it was clear that Fitterer had lost control of the university.

It takes great provocation for one Jesuit to act against another, especially an administrative superior. This is both a strength and a weakness of the hierarchical structure established by St. Ignatius and maintained over hundreds of years, and it explains why no one challenged Fitterer's leadership as the university careened toward a financial precipice.

Fitterer had also done his best to conceal or rationalize the school's plummeting fortunes, but when the Robertson revelations made the crisis front page news, the university's Jesuit trustees could delay action no longer. They appealed directly to Father Small, who was the highest ranking Jesuit in America at the time, and even to Rome for the Superior General's intercession.

The opening of the Connolly Center on November 7, 1969, proved to be Father Fitterer's final ceremony as president. A week later his vice president for finance revealed that Seattle University had slid $1 million deeper into debt during the current year and enrollment had sunk below 3,500. At their meeting on December 12, 1969, the trustees voted to scrap the Seattle Plan which Fitterer had unveiled only five years earlier. The new Core Curriculum was slashed to 65 credits, and five credit hours were restored for each course commencing in the new school year. Two weeks later, Fitterer submitted his resignation.

In the spring of 1966, it seemed that Father Fitterer had taken the wheel of a race car on a fast track to certain success. In reality, Seattle University was running out of gas before the end of Lemieux's presidency, but Fitterer never took his foot off the pedal. Worse, he charged every financial refill on a credit card that was already over its limit.

Now the university was skidding dangerously close to a cliff — and the next driver was about to make a sudden right turn.

Fr. Fitterer's good intentions in promising public access to the new Connolly Center only paved the way to future controversy. As he and Archbishop Connolly broke ground for the new gym, few knew that the university was digging its own financial grave.

Overleaf: Anti-war demonstrators protest the invasion of Cambodia in front of Lemieux Library, May 15, 1970.

Inset: The university's shrinking enrollment gave this greeting on a restaurant reader board an ironic twist.

TO THE BRINK AND BACK

Seattle University was introduced to its new president, Father Kenneth Baker, SJ, at a press conference on January 7, 1970. He had already taken his seat on the Board of Trustees five days earlier, replacing Father Robert Rebhahn, SJ.

Born in Tacoma and educated at Gonzaga, Baker earned his doctorate in religious studies at Marquette before returning to Spokane to teach theology. When that campus became embroiled in disputes over student morals and academic reform, Baker earned a reputation as an effective champion of orthodoxy. He even impressed Superior General Arrupe, a liberal who nonetheless agreed with local Jesuits that Baker was the right man to restore order to Seattle University.

At that same press conference on January 7, the new executive vice president Father Perri lavished praise on Fitterer and announced that he would serve as the university's first Chancellor, a new post responsible for fund raising. It was a strange assignment given Fitterer's track record, but the real purpose was to save face for Fitterer and the school, and perhaps, to restore calm after the Jesuit equivalent of a coup d'etat.

Baker held strong views on education, especially Catholic education which he felt was drifting away from its spiritual and doctrinal center. For his part, Baker promised "flexibility" and respect for the "norms of dissent." He add-

ed, "If students come in and sit down and tell me they are not going to leave until I talk to them, then I'll go out and talk to them. I think that if you're willing to listen, most things can be worked out." These words would come back to haunt him five months later.

Before he could deal with ideology, however, Baker had to contend with the university's worsening finances. He pressed ahead with the new Core Curriculum and began trimming staff. He soon reported that the $1.4 million operating deficit had been halved. In his most durable contribution to the university, Baker also began the process of drafting new bylaws for lay representation on the Board of Trustees.

The racial climate was still unsettled. The Black Student Union demanded $1,500 from the ASSU for a separate Black homecoming. When the ASSU offered a lesser sum, the BSU spurned it and threatened a boycott by African-American basketball players. This fizzled, but a real bomb detonated between Garrand and the Lib-

eral Arts (now Administration) Building on the night of January 19, shattering windows throughout campus. No one claimed responsibility and the perpetrators were never identified.

Baker came under direct attack in early March when minority affairs director Charles Mitchell blasted him for a tepid commitment to affirmative action in faculty hiring. At the same moment, William Cooley, who chaired the faculty's urban affairs committee, claimed that the campus was "permeated by racism." Baker angrily rejected both charges.

By spring, the "reductions in force" were also causing tensions on the faculty. This became critical in the case of Rabbi Jacobovitz, who had been informed the previous November that in order to save funds, he would not be renewed as a lecturer. Jacobovitz's role on campus had grown from making an annual presentation to Father Thomas O'Brien's honors program into a regular course in the theology department, now headed by Father LeRoux. His teaching also evolved from Hebrew scholarship into projects in which his students donned yarmulkes and lived for weeks like orthodox Jews. In the process Jacobovitz managed to rankle not only some Catholics but also liberal members of the Jewish community, many of whom were supporters of Seattle University.

The financial emergency seemed to offer the administration an opportune excuse to dispense with Jacobovitz, although his annual com-

The university's ROTC program inspired repeated and increasingly violent protests during May 1970. Emile Wilson was the only Seattle University student arrested after demonstrators vandalized the Chieftain.

pensation was only $1,000. Jacobovitz responded by offering to lecture at no charge, an idea which was spurned during a traumatic interview with Fitterer. Unaware of all the complexities, many saw the incident in terms of a conservative religious retrenchment. The Faculty Senate and more than 1,000 students petitioned for Jacobovitz's reinstatement, which LeRoux approved in mid-April, and Rabbi Jacobovitz still lectures at Seattle University.

Baker, unfortunately, picked this same moment to speculate publicly about terminating the basketball program and changing the school's name to "Seattle Jesuit University" to "heighten its Jesuit identity." As Jean Merlino, university publicist at the time, recalls, "You just couldn't tell him to keep his mouth shut." The mounting confusion led *Seattle Magazine*, a slick urban monthly subsidized by KING Broadcasting, to decry "The Waning of Seattle University" in its April edition (ironically, one of the magazine's last).

Baker set more teeth on edge when he welcomed Senator Barry Goldwater to campus for a speaking engagement at the end of March. That same week unknown intruders set a fire in Xavier Hall. Security guards, whom Baker had just introduced on campus, fired on the fleeing arsonists without apparent effect.

Days later, President Nixon sent American troops into Cambodia, which he had been secretly bombing for months. Campuses across the nation rose up in angry protests and strikes. On May 4, 1970, Ohio National Guardsmen killed four demonstrators on the campus of Kent State University. Over the following days, eight more students — all African-Americans — were killed in demonstrations on southern university campuses.

The entire nation was shocked, and Father Baker sent a telegram to Nixon asking him to "restore the nation's conscience." A new Student Coalition demanded that Baker discon-

tinue the ROTC program and threatened to occupy his office if he didn't. Baker replied that if
they did, he would call the police and have them
arrested. Nothing happened that day, but Baker
was eyeball to eyeball with his critics and he
was determined not to blink.

Just when tensions were at their highest,
the new head of the sociology department, Anita
Yourglich, made a fateful decision. In filling an
interim vacancy, she had winnowed the appli-
cants down to two men: Ray Napierkowski, who
had graduated with honors from Seattle University in 1969, and William Hodge, an African-
American teaching assistant recruited from the
University of Washington by Charles Mitchell
expressly at the department's request. Yourglich
chose Napierkowski for his stronger background
in research and statistics. The administration
tried quietly to get Yourglich to reconsider, but
she stood on what she regarded as solid academic ground. This crumbled beneath her when
the *Spectator* published a memorandum in which
Yourglich appeared to disavow any need for her
department or the university to achieve racial
balance on the faculty.

On May 15, some 150 protesters (many of
whom were not Seattle University students)
marched on campus demanding that Hodge be
hired and that the ROTC program be kicked off
campus. Baker met with the students and after
much shouting the two sides parted. Three days
later, on Monday, May 18, Baker issued new
rules banning demonstrations without advance
administration approval. This inflamed tempers
anew, and a second group of 150 marched to the
Liberal Arts Building. This time, Baker refused
to speak to them, despite the best efforts of
Charles Mitchell to moderate the dispute, and
several students invaded the president's office.
During the ensuing melee of shouts and waving
fists a table was overturned, a lamp destroyed
and books knocked from their shelves, but no
blows were exchanged.

After leaving the building, the students re-
treated to the nearby Seattle Central Community College where their ranks swelled with another 100 students and miscellaneous demonstrators. The group marched back to Seattle
University, chanting "Shut it down!" Protesters
entered Pigott Hall, and scuffled with students
and the police TAC Squad, and scattered.

Still fuming from the invasion of his office,
Baker conducted an impromptu press conference on campus. He stated that six students had
held him "captive" and they would be suspended. He went on to declare that he would not
allow protestors to "break SU so we'll have to
turn it over to the state [and] make it a black
university." Baker vowed that he would "not
tolerate anarchical activity on campus. This is a
return to the jungle." He warned that those
attempting to "change us to service black political needs" would be "on a head-on collision
course." Baker concluded by challenging the
news media to "size this up for what it is, an-
archy and fascism, and turn your guns on them."
Baker's words were broadcast far and wide, and
he received an avalanche of mail in response —
almost all of it supportive. He also received
anonymous threats which were taken seriously
enough for the police to assign two plainclothes
officers to protect Baker around the clock, even
standing guard outside his Loyola apartment.

While many of his colleagues and university
supporters may have agreed privately with
Baker, they were alarmed by the intemperance
of his public remarks. As Father Sauvain later
put it, Baker displayed "more sandpaper than
velvet." Although only a tiny percentage of the
total student population had participated in
events to date, the entire campus was caught in
the cross-fire and anxieties were mounting by
the minute.

The following day, May 19, Baker suspended five students for invading his office: Emile
Wilson, Bobby Davis, Eddie Leon, Pete Orange,
and Doug Yackulic. That evening, the Faculty
Senate and ASSU Senate held a joint session

*Charles Mitchell and
Anita Yourglich (top)
clashed over affirmative
action for the sociology
department. Fr. Kenneth
Baker, SJ, greets Senator
Barry Goldwater, whose
visit in April 1970 fueled
more political tension.*

during which a motion of "no confidence" in Baker's presidency was narrowly defeated.

On Wednesday, May 20, the Student Afro-American Movement for Equality (formerly the BSU) held a noon rally which attracted upwards of 300, including off-campus activists. His temper cooled, Baker spoke to the group and withstood catcalls and hostile questions, but nothing worse. Many credit Father McGoldrick for defusing the situation. As Father Gaffney recalls, "Father McGoldrick had his greatest day when someone made the mistake of handing him the microphone" to address the library rally. The crowd dissolved peaceably, but later that afternoon a small gang of protesters rampaged through the Chieftain, smashing several windows. The police waded in and arrested six, of whom only one was African-American or a Seattle University student, Emile Wilson. The charges were later dropped.

Baker's suspensions of Wilson and the other students accused of invading his office were taken up by the Student Conduct Review Board on May 27. The panel was chaired by Father Rebhahn, vice president for students. Its members included Agnes Reilly, dean of women, Father Sauvain, chaplain, and Ben Cashman, chairman of political science and the AAUP representative, and two ASSU officers. The Board's rulings were advisory to the president, but Baker, feeling he was too personally involved, asked Father McGoldrick to make the final determination.

After four hours of hearings, during which Baker was questioned closely by the defendants and panel, and three hours of deliberation, the Board voted to reinstate all five students. Doug Yackulic was exonerated as a victim of misidentification, and the other four were placed on probation in the judgment that while something had happened in Baker's office and they were participants, events were too confused to assign precise blame. Father Baker apologized to Yackulic for implicating him by error, and the incident

was closed. The next day, classes were suspended for "rap sessions" and peace-making. Mercifully, the spring quarter ended without further disturbances.

As a postscript it should be noted that Ray Napierkowski, the man whose selection had triggered two weeks of turmoil, was never actually hired. The position remained empty for a year until the Reverend Joe Mills, an Episcopal priest, was quietly appointed; Napierkowski later returned to campus to earn a doctorate in education.

During the summer of 1970, Father Cronin was named vice president for students and Father Morton vacated the academic vice presidency to become the Oregon provincial's assistant for education. Father Gaffney was tapped as the new academic vice president, and the entire administration turned its attention back to finances. They were worse than ever in late September 1970, when Baker offered a public accounting of the university's situation. He reported that the school was still running $1 million in the red, despite a new $480,000 loan against which the university had pledged its Ford Foundation grant income. Baker blamed sagging enrollment, and he publicly acknowledged that the cost of building Connolly Center was "a sacrifice to our actual and potential financial stability."

Seattle was now in the grip of the "Boeing Bust." The recession meant there was little prospect for outside financial aid for the college and fewer families which could afford Seattle University. Despite this, Baker almost doubled tuition for the coming year to $510 per quarter and he announced yet another $5 million fund drive under Father Fitterer's direction.

Nothing came of this, and much more interest was generated by a mysterious trip Baker had taken in September to Rome. Reports were confused as to whether Baker was seeking Church intervention, negotiating a financial bail-

out, or just sightseeing. Baker did little to clear up the matter, saying "I went to Rome to talk to people, not to visit monuments." Among these people were the controversial author Gore Vidal and a Middle Eastern ambassador to the Vatican. A newspaper photo of Baker chatting amiably with Vidal, an avowed bisexual, angered conservatives, and Baker didn't help his cause with other university benefactors when he told the *Spectator* that the Arab point of view was "not given fair press in America."

This controversy was still smoldering in October when Baker rekindled the flames of the previous spring by issuing new rules that gave the president unlimited power to suspend or expel students at "his sole discretion." A week after this pronouncement, he froze all expenditures as a "precautionary measure." Enrollment continued to plummet, and Eddie Cotton's restaurant up on Madison posted a greeting on its reader board: "Welcome SU Student." The *Spectator* joked that it wasn't "quite that bad." In fact, it was worse.

On October 10, Baker and key officials traveled to Yakima's Chinook Hotel where they met behind closed doors with their opposite numbers from Gonzaga and the new Oregon provincial, Father Kenneth J. Galbraith. As Father Gaffney later recalled, "The agenda was which college to close, and Gonzaga was already dividing up our faculty." Baker laid out the options for the university: bankruptcy, lease or sale to the state, or trying to hold the line a little longer. Galbraith endorsed the last approach.

Galbraith subsequently reported to Rome that the regents made it clear to him that their support "required that the Catholic dimension be played down and the Christian humanism aspect be played up," contrary to Baker's views. The regents had reached the end of their tether. They held an unprecedented joint meeting with Baker and the trustees on October 23 at which it was revealed that the university could not meet the following week's payroll. It was agreed that the university should immediately seek a moratorium on its federal loan payments, but the regents wanted action of a different sort.

William Jenkins, president of Seafirst Bank, insisted that "the university must balance its budget." Leslie Sheridan chastised Baker to "take greater care in the public statements of the president." Regents chairman Bob O'Brien demanded a "change in leadership since the latter was clearly in disarray." He proposed that Lemieux should take over as Chancellor and "chief executive officer," replacing Fitterer and severely curtailing Baker's power as president. Fitterer resigned the following day, but Baker tried to salvage his presidency. Galbraith met selected regents and the Board of Trustees on October 25, at which time Baker argued that he should retain control while promising to screen future public pronouncements.

The Jesuit trustees reluctantly concluded that it wasn't enough. One of them, Father Frank Wood, who had sought Baker's appointment so eagerly less than a year before, now realized that "he would have been a great president — forty years ago. The Lord just did not give him the art of diplomacy." Forcing Baker's removal was a wrenching decision nonetheless, and Wood "prayed more than I ever had before." It fell to him to communicate the trustees' verdict to Baker. "I did what I had to do," Wood says, "I just did it." Galbraith later recounted, "Feeling on the issue [of Baker] ran so strong that I was urged to step into the picture and settle the issues immediately lest we not only lose the University but a Jesuit community as well."

On October 27, Baker publicly called for a 10 percent budget cut. "Our backs are against the wall," he declared. "Certain decisions must be made to keep the university viable." Those decisions were made at a day-long emergency meeting on October 30, attended by Galbraith, Baker, selected regents and the Board of Trustees. Lemieux reported that his health would

not permit him to take charge of the university, which foreclosed the last option for preserving a semblance of Baker's presidency. There was only one course of action left, and in Galbraith's words, "Father Baker, in a generous fashion typical of him, accepted their decision and tendered his resignation."

On the following day, the trustees made Father Gaffney acting president. Regent William Woods demanded the replacement of Elliott Paulson as development director, and Bill Boeing agreed to co-chair an intensive "stabilization" fund drive with Lemieux. Bob O'Brien and other regents later pledged their own credit to meet the university's immediate payroll and operating costs.

Father Baker penned a letter of resignation on November 1, 1970, in which he found a voice that might have prevented disaster had he used it earlier:

Dear Students:

By the time you read these words you will all be aware of my resignation from the presidency of Seattle University. I have tried my best to understand you and to work for your interests in every way I could. I deeply appreciate the many kindnesses you have shown me; the opposition I expected, since it goes with the position — and it forces all of us to grow just a little more.

I leave Seattle U. with great affection for the high-quality student body. Although I have had differences with some of you, I respect you and admire the maturity that has been developed here over the years. In the future I will follow with interest the growth of Seattle University. May God be with you all.

> *Yours very sincerely,*
> *Kenneth Baker, S.J.*

By the time this letter was released, Baker and Fitterer were gone, both officially "on vacation." Rome accepted the fait accompli pre-

William Woods joined other regents in demanding an overhaul of the university administration. Oregon Provincial Kenneth Galbraith, SJ, intervened "lest we not only lose the university but a Jesuit community as well." Fr. Baker accepted his colleagues' judgment and resigned "in a generous fashion typical of him."

Students, faculty and staff convene on November 2, 1970, to hear their new president, Fr. Louis Gaffney, SJ, prescribe "contagious optimism" to heal the university's wounds.

sented by the Seattle trustees and the provincial. Ken Baker returned to his studies and became editor of a scholarly Catholic journal. The Society of Jesus assigned Jack Fitterer to Washington, DC, where he ably headed the Association of Jesuit Colleges and Universities for several years. Ultimately, he drifted away from the Society and the Catholic Church, married and took up an Episcopalian ministry in California.

On November 2, Father Gaffney summoned the students and faculty to an emergency convocation in the Connolly Gym. The entire college gave a standing ovation when Gaffney was introduced as their acting president and he gave them a rousing pep talk in return.

"Contagious optimism will give us the energy to close ranks," he preached, "We shall make it!" Putting the past few months of turmoil to rest, Gaffney pledged, "The president and trustees will take every step to protect students and their rights. You will always be treated graciously and with consideration." Gaffney announced that Father Lemieux and Bill Boeing were jointly launching a "stabilization drive" to raise $3 million. A few days later, Bill Guppy became the university's first lay academic vice president and Gaffney picked a retired Navy admiral, George Towner, to be his own administrative assistant.

"Contagious optimism" became the rallying cry throughout campus, but financial realism was the first order of business for Gaffney and his administration. On November 25, 1970, the board approved an average 8 percent cut in salaries, a $200,000 reduction in administrative overhead, suspension of the major in Physics, a reorganization of Computer Center staffing, and negotiation of a moratorium on all federal loan payments. They cut the budget by 10 percent across the board and increased professors' average class loads from 35 to 40 credits per year. At least on paper, these moves erased a projected half million dollar deficit for the current fiscal year.

Marycrest was leased out for a convalescent home, and miscellaneous properties were sold while the university's few remaining unencumbered assets were pledged for a new bridge loan to cover expenses. Efforts to preserve use of Campion Hall were abandoned and it closed while Bellarmine went co-ed, and Xavier was transformed back into a men's dorm.

Reforms continued apace in the new year. The most significant and controversial move was taken in January 1971. Mathematics, biology and the physical sciences were shifted from the School of Arts and Sciences to the School of Engineering under Dean Dr. David Schroeder. The result was called the School of Science and Technology (or "SST" for short) until March, when the School of Science and Engineering was formally approved. Some professors grumbled about lack of consultation but Gaffney did not waver, insisting that a shotgun marriage was the only way to save both physical sciences and engineering at the university. Father Bradley stepped down as Arts and Sciences dean in April 1971 and Father Royce took the reins.

Pay cuts, layoffs, hiring freezes, budget cuts, and a temporary suspension of new tenure added to strains on campus but the university community held together. No one had joined the Seattle University faculty with the idea of getting rich. Lay instructors and professors were attracted instead by the opportunity to focus on teaching without the pressures for winning grants or publishing which burdened the faculty of a research university. Lay members were also drawn to the university by a commitment to a special set of values, if not a shared religion.

Many professors volunteered for salary cuts to spare needier colleagues and improvised cost savings of their own. Members of the engineering faculty worked out a rotation plan with local companies so they could take "sabbaticals" in industry to relieve the financial burden on their departments. Others learned how to repackage their material to increase student interest. Dr. John Toutonghi, for example, reinvigorated lagging interest in physics by offering a popular new class in astronomy. When all else failed, many lay professors taught their courses without compensation. For their part, Jesuit faculty members had donated their official salaries back to the university since the school's founding.

Their sacrifices were not wasted. Thanks to faculty efforts, rising tuition income, a partial moratorium on federal debt, and over three-quarters of a million dollars in contributions solicited by Father Lemieux and Bill Boeing, the university was able to close the books on fiscal year 1971 in July with $95,000 left over. The institution was still buried up to its institutional nostrils in debt, but it had stopped sinking.

As it mastered its finances, the university also learned to master the changes which continued to buffet it and the larger community. The Vietnam War was still raging and it produced the university's first Congressional Medal of Honor winner, Major Patrick Brady (class of '59), and claimed the university's first combat death, Lt. Duane Cordiner, a 1969 graduate. The war also took its toll on the ROTC program, which shrank from 150 members in 1969 to 60 by the end of 1971. Establishment of a draft counseling center on campus in 1970 and ASSU's formal endorsement of national peace protests in May 1971 signalled deepening disenchantment with the war in Vietnam.

Women's Liberation made its debut on campus as female students pressed for more services and a stronger voice in campus government. The *Spectator* broke down an ancient male stronghold by naming a woman, Sue Hill, as sports editor in 1970. Dwindling registrations led to phasing out Home Economics and Secretarial Studies (although budget savings were the proximate cause of their demise).

Emile Wilson returned for a fifth year in the fall of 1971 and was elected ASSU Publicity Director. The campus also welcomed back Ed O'Brien as athletic director. He had just taken a year's sabbatical coaching for the Pilots, Seattle's original, short-lived American League franchise. The Seattle Supersonics' new star, Spencer Haywood, transferred from the University of Detroit to finish his senior year. The Chieftains must have regretted that Haywood was ineligible to play for them as they stumbled through their worst season in two decades.

Gaffney expanded staffing for minority affairs as students of Asian and Hispanic descent became more vocal in demanding recognition and rights. The present McGoldrick Center was purchased and the former Jesuit residences which then housed faculty offices and the *Aegis* and *Spectator* were demolished — no reflection on their editorial content was intended.

Gaffney was officially named president on November 4, 1971, with the private stipulation that he be relieved of the post within five years. On that day, he unveiled an entirely new structure for university governance under a 13-member board including both Jesuits and lay men and women. These trustees would be named by a new "membership board," of nine Jesuits, essentially a holding company.

On November 12, 1971, Gaffney presented the new Board of Trustees to the campus (in addition to himself as president and in alphabetical order): former Chieftain great Elgin Baylor; Bill Boeing; boat yard owner Jon Bowman; philosophy professor and former trustee Father

Bob O'Brien took the reins as chair of the university's first Board of Trustees to include lay members.

Bill Guppy became the first layman to serve as academic vice president.

Dr. David Schroeder assembled the new School of Science and Engineering.

Marguerite Casey offered $1 million if the university could raise $2 million. Eva Albers satisfied the Casey challenge when she left an estate establishing a $3 million endowment for the university.

Leo Kaufman, SJ; Seattle Prep principal Father John Kindall, SJ; former academic vice president Father Edmund Morton, SJ, now assistant for education to the Oregon provincial; Seattle University alumna, former Guild president and Everett Community College trustee Anne Nelskog; former regents' president Bob O'Brien, who would become the first chairman of the new Board; Mount St. Michael Seminary's rector Father Patrick O'Leary, SJ; Everett Community College president Jeanette Poore; music professor Father Kevin Waters, SJ; and engineering professor and long-time trustee, Father Frank Wood.

Father Gaffney concluded his introductions and appealed for everyone's support. "As we begin what might be called a new era in Seattle University history, there are many things which we must seek to accomplish. First of all we must deepen and ennoble the great pride we have in one another and in our University. We must be enthusiastic, optimistic as we strive for our common goals..."

The new year began with the hiring of Mick McHugh as alumni director. The university's fund raising suddenly faced a new but not unwelcome challenge when Marguerite Casey wrote to Bob O'Brien on January 6, 1971. Insisting on anonymity at the time, she and her family offered to donate $1 million if $2 million more were raised in two years. The university met and exceeded this challenge in May thanks to the extraordinary generosity of Mrs. Eva Albers, whose estate established a $3 million endowment. Her daughter and executrix, Genevieve Albers, gave credit for the gift to Father Lemieux, who had enlisted Eva Albers as one of the first members of the university's Women's Guild. Genevieve Albers later joined the Board of Trustees and remains one of the university's most dedicated champions. In recognition, the School of Business and Economics now bears her family name.

Fulfilling her part of the bargain, Marguerite Casey promptly transferred 87,000 shares of United Parcel Service, which had been founded by her brother James, a long-time friend of the university. This was used to establish the George W. Casey Endowment in their father's name.

Also that spring, the university launched a new effort to secure research grants under the direction of Father Cowgill. He in turn enlisted the aid of Gary Zimmerman, a chemist who spurred development of the university's pioneering medical technology curriculum and garnered one of only two national grants for work in diagnostic ultrasound. The university's scientific reputation was also buoyed by Drs. Don Malins and Usha Varanasi's pathfinding research in the physiology of dolphin sonar.

The campus turbulence of previous years was not quite spent. At 3:15 am on May 6, 1972, a large bomb exploded beneath the steps of the ROTC building with such force that it blew out every window in the facing side of Loyola Hall. Miraculously, no one was injured. A bomb of a different sort went off when the Chieftains fin-

ished their first losing season since 1950. Coach Morris "Bucky" Buckwalter left for the Sonics' staff (and a much better record in pro basketball) and was replaced with Bill O'Connor.

The fall of 1972 saw enrollment sink to a new low of 2,856. The faculty shrank to 149, a decline of 13 percent from the previous school year. Any anxiety this might have caused did not translate into support for collective bargaining as faculty members rejected union representation by the AAUP by a vote of 76 to 53. Gaffney pursued his reforms by adding Ethnic Study courses to the Core Curriculum and establishing the first affirmative action plan for university hiring. More staff changes were made during the academic year as Eugene Corr, former Assistant Chief of the Seattle Police, took over the innovative Community Services Degree program from the ailing Naomi Goodard, John Morford succeeded Winfield Fountain as dean of Education, Gary Zimmerman took over as dean of Science and Engineering, and Judge Charles Z. Smith joined the trustees in place of Elgin Baylor. Father James Powers, SJ, succeeded Father Royce as dean of Arts and Sciences and replaced Father Wood as a trustee.

As the school year drew to a close in May 1973, the State Supreme Court dealt the university a body blow by declaring state aid to students of religiously affiliated institutions unconstitutional. With tuition at $560 a quarter and room and board at over $2,700 a year, every cent of financial assistance was critical. Despite the loss of state funds for students, enrollment rebounded by 10 percent to 3,120 in the fall of 1973, rising for the first time in nine years. Gaffney implemented a modest but still welcome 5 percent pay raise, and pressed ahead with more reforms. He began leasing floors of Campion to community agencies, established a day care center, and most significant of all, authorized planning for a radical new program which condensed high school and college studies into a single six-year curriculum.

This idea had been circulating in one form or another since the early 1940s, when Father McGoldrick joined educational reformers Robert Hutchins and Mortimer Adler in advocating an accelerated path from high school to a baccalaureate degree. The Carnegie Commission had renewed discussion of the concept in calling for educational reforms in the early 1970s and Seattle University faculty had explored the idea during a brainstorming retreat at the Battelle Institute in 1972. The real impetus for what would become Matteo Ricci College, however, had nothing to do with any of these exercises.

As Gaffney later recalled, Oregon provincial Galbraith and his key advisers visited Loyola Hall in the winter of 1973 and "amazed" the assembled Jesuits with the news that Seattle Prep "had been singled out for a special experiment. It was to become a new type of school or 'die,' that is, the provincial would send no more Jesuits to support it." In essence, Galbraith believed that the Jesuits had a higher mission than teaching the children of affluent Catholics. He wanted Prep to do more for society.

The precise character of the new school was unclear to Galbraith's audience, Gaffney remembers, "except that it was to emphasize a 'social apostolate' and Seattle Prep would be restructured by a group of five young Jesuits." This "core group" was composed of Fathers Greg Steiner, Rich Perry, Rick Miranda, and John Foster (the only Prep teacher in the cadre) and headed by Father Tom Healy. The real mission and the ultimatum behind their efforts were not discussed beyond the Jesuit community. Seattle University's confidence in this experiment was not high, but the provincial's warning that, in Gaffney's words, "Seattle Prep must change or wither away" was taken very seriously. A successful Jesuit high school in Mexico City had just paid this price for failing to meet such a challenge. When Galbraith made the plan public in May 1973, he conceded it was a "leap

in the dark," and "the riskiest thing the province has done since I don't know when."

Initial discussions of how to realize the provincial's mandate for a social apostolate in a high school proved inconclusive. In January 1974, Father Powers steered the effort toward development of a "six-year continuum" of education leading to a bachelor's degree. In this way, a more concrete educational agenda supplanted the social mission while maintaining an innovative, if not revolutionary course. Powers' March 1974 report to the Seattle University trustees outlined a new "Seattle Preparatory College" designed "to foster a new catholic spirit of wonder and its manifest dimensions through an integrated and interdisciplinary course of studies." Turning these lofty words into the flesh of a functional school by 1975 fell to Father LeRoux and an expanded planning task force.

The new college was not the only academic enterprise facing Gaffney and his administration. Bill Guppy and Gary Zimmerman devoted over a year to researching creation of a School of Optometry before the plan had to be abandoned owing to lack of funding. Efforts were more successful in forging a "consortium" with Washington State University for new classes in hotel and restaurant management on Seattle's campus. The greatest success was a new masters program in public administration which attracted 99 students the following fall. The greatest challenge was posed by the engineering courses, which were suffering from outdated equipment and an overworked faculty. Civil engineering lost its accreditation in the spring of 1974 and the balance of engineering programs were put on probation for two years.

Progress continued on the social front as Seattle University implemented a holiday honoring the birthday of Dr. Martin Luther King Jr. and formally joined the boycott of non-union grapes and lettuce sponsored by the United Farm Workers. The union's leader, Cesar Chavez, was a frequent campus visitor. In Feb-

ruary 1974, the university rolled out the red carpet for Dave Barrett, British Columbia's socialist premiere and a member of the class of 1953.

By then Gaffney was in the fourth year of his self-imposed five-year tenure as president. On June 4, 1974, Gaffney tendered his resignation to the trustees effective a year hence if a new president were not named earlier.

Father Gaffney's mission had been accomplished. Like a paramedic on the scene of an automobile accident, he had worked swiftly to stabilize the university and bind its wounds. Four years after its worst crisis, the university was on the mend thanks to the miraculous serum of Gaffney's own contagious optimism. It was now time for others to take over the university's care, but there was one more complication to come.

Genevieve Albers built upon her mother's bequest with her own leadership as a trustee and benefactor.

Overleaf: Fr. William Sullivan, SJ, enlisted Fr. Lemieux as the university's Chancellor to help foster the university's renaissance.

Inset: Emile Wilson became the university's first Rhodes Scholar under the tutelage of Fr. McGoldrick.

XI

CHANGE AND CONTINUITY

uring the winter of 1974, the Board of Trustees debated the question of whether or not Gaffney's successor need be a Jesuit. The issue became moot when the presidential search committee narrowed its list of candidates to two, Fathers Robert Weiss and Edmund Ryan, both members of the Society of Jesus.

The latter had already made a reputation for himself as an innovative educator at Georgetown University, and Ryan was clearly eager to pursue his career at Seattle University. Ryan was also a master of politics and the media. He projected a captivating intelligence in person and on camera, and during the evaluation process, Ryan spent a great deal of time in the area courting trustees and university supporters. Weiss recognized the inevitable outcome and withdrew his name from consideration in December 1974.

The selection of Ryan was announced on January 24, 1975. On that same day, Emile Wilson was named Seattle University's first Rhodes Scholar. President Baker's former antagonist had been taken under wing by Father McGoldrick and was now completing his master's degree in education. More good news arrived as winter enrollment jumped more than 14 percent to 3,559 and graduate student enrollment grew by a remarkable 70 percent. This created the largest fall registration since 1966, notwithstanding a rise in tuition to $1,960 a year.

It seemed that the university had survived

its political, financial and administrative crises. Everyone eagerly looked forward to the spring when Father Ryan would formally assume the presidency. Ryan did not disappoint campus expectations for a vigorous presidency. Upon taking office, he declared, "To all of you I pledge my complete dedication, my every fiber, my every waking hour." These were not hollow words, and Ryan established office hours in Bellarmine to demonstrate his accessibility and commitment.

At his first meeting with the trustees on April 7, Ryan outlined a complete reorganization of his administration with the creation of an assistant to the president for planning, an executive vice president, and a provost to guide academic development. For this last position, he already had a candidate in mind, Father William J. Sullivan, SJ.

A theologian trained in France and Germany, Sullivan took his doctorate at Yale and taught at Marquette before being named dean of Divinity at St. Louis University. The program

was, he recalls, a "total shambles." In the process of rebuilding the School of Divinity, Sullivan developed close relations with the nearby Lutheran seminary, Concordia. When that school was ripped asunder by doctrinal warfare and the entire faculty was sacked, Sullivan invited unemployed teachers and striking students to relocate on his campus in 1974. The transplanted Lutherans became known as the "Seminary in Exile," or "Seminex" for short.

For some Church officials, this was carrying ecumenism too far. The divinity school was reorganized out of existence and Sullivan resigned in January 1975. Ryan promptly approached him about the Provost position and Sullivan visited Seattle in April, at which time he praised the university's "reputation for being a school working hard at the role of an urban university." Sullivan returned in August to become Seattle University's first provost.

Ryan wasted no time getting to work. He reviewed his faculty and staff and decided to replace 32 in his first six weeks. In the process, Ryan demanded strict departmental adherence to affirmative action requirements. The results, however, would continue to fall short of expectations for racial progress since Seattle University lacked the resources to compete with larger institutions for available minority scholars and educators.

Ryan aggressively campaigned through the spring for funding to launch the new six-year

Fr. Edmund Ryan, SJ, inspired expectations for change during his brief presidency. Dr. Virginia Parks was tapped by Fr. Sullivan to unravel the university's books as the first woman vice president for finance.

college, now named for Matteo Ricci, the pioneering 16th century Jesuit scientist and missionary to China. This program had evolved dramatically over the past year. Rather than merely telescoping a conventional eight-year path from high school to a bachelor's degree into six, planners redesigned secondary and college education from scratch. Dr. Bernard Steckler, who now directs the Form II portion of the program at the university (Form I being the Seattle Prep phase), recalls that the task force centered its efforts on the idea that "I learn because we learn and what we know depends on how we know." The resulting program broke down the traditional hierarchy between students and faculty and introduced a radical concept of participatory and interdisciplinary education.

The entire Seattle Prep curriculum was reorganized on this principle and became co-educational. The experiment was funded in June 1975 with a Carnegie grant of nearly a quarter of a million dollars, secured through Ryan's efforts. Father Healy took the helm at Seattle Prep and prepared to welcome the first Form I students that fall. That same June, Swedish Hospital expressed interest in purchasing Marycrest. The trustees were happy to talk and planned to use the sale proceeds to pay off the lingering Ziegler debt, but it would not prove quite so simple.

Ryan's foremost interest, to the point of obsession, was passage of House Joint Resolution 19 amending the state constitution to permit public funds to be granted to schools with religious affiliations. The previous attempt to accomplish this by legislation had run afoul of the state supreme court. Ryan lobbied the legislature to get the measure on the ballot, but voters soundly rejected the measure that fall, and Ryan seemed to take it personally. Events dealt another disappointment in the fall of 1975, when enrollment dropped by 434 registrations. Some blamed this on a tuition increase to $720 per quarter,

which had been approved as one of Father Gaffney's last acts. It saved his successor the heat of raising fees, but not the grief.

Otherwise, the 1975/76 year started out fairly typically with its share of ups and downs. Seattle Prep launched Matteo Ricci College with 150 students and Father Sullivan took office as provost. At his first meeting with trustees, Sullivan outlined an ambitious mission to "coordinate between the academic area and students, [initiate] long-range planning, and develop supporting programs." He also assumed responsibility for preparing the university to greet its first Matteo Ricci Form II students three years hence and for implementing new master's degree programs in accounting and rehabilitation services.

Such progress was momentarily eclipsed when Joe Gallucci, a popular instructor and alumnus, angrily resigned over perceived mistreatment of the fine arts department. The Minority Affairs office became embroiled in a tug of war between African-Americans, Latino and Asian-American students. Ryan squandered his popularity with students when he tried to pressure the *Spectator* into publishing a special section on an upcoming business seminar. He undercut his credibility with trustees by authorizing an expensive remodeling of administrative offices — complete with wet bar for the president's office (since removed) — when the university was still scratching its way back to solvency.

Ryan had attempted to involve himself in every facet of university life and every decision affecting it, but he seemed to be losing his sense of priorities. The physical and psychological toll was obvious by November, and on January 14, 1976, Ryan checked into Providence Hospital suffering from "fatigue and a viral infection." Ryan returned briefly a few weeks later, but he was clearly in a state of mental exhaustion. Finally, trustees' chairman Robert O'Brien took him aside and asked him to leave for the sake of his own health and the university's. Ryan agreed on February 27, 1976. After recuperating in Tacoma, he returned to the east and later joined the adminstration of a small Jesuit college in upper New York State.

During Father Ryan's illness, Father Sullivan had become de facto president and impressed everyone with his energy and skill. The trustees conducted a pro forma search for a new president, but their selection was a foregone conclusion. On May 3, 1976, Father William Sullivan became Seattle University's 20th president.

Shortly before that date, while still acting president, Sullivan addressed a spring convocation of faculty and staff. He began by acknowledging Father Ryan, "a person who is absent today. My gratitude, and I think our gratitude, [is owed] to a brilliant and energetic man who came into our midst a year ago and brought both a vision and an understanding of what Seattle University really is and could be." Sullivan continued by outlining his view of the university's mission in education and service to society, a theme to which he would return at every succeeding convocation, but morale was his paramount concern. He closed with a line from Dostoevsky, "...Whatever the future holds, let us remember these days when we are together now united in a common task with a common spirit, which makes each of us greater than he [or she] is."

Since he had really been performing the president's duties for many months, Father Sullivan hit the ground running in May. He acted quickly to launch the "CORPUS" program for lay ministers and a masters program for pastoral ministry under the direction of Dr. Leo Stanford, whom he recruited from St. Louis, and to develop the McGoldrick Center as a home for student services.

More important than these specific initiatives, Sullivan introduced a new, more corporate style to the presidency, and soon organized a cabinet of key administrators to improve communication and systematize university management. In this undertaking, Sullivan's foremost preoccupation was the university's budget, which had drifted $200,000 into the red. His first official act was to name accounting professor Dr. Virginia Parks as his financial vice president, giving her the distinction of being the first woman to occupy a top administrative post. With this honor came the thankless responsibility for solving the university's most intractable problem.

Parks burrowed into the university books and was horrified by what she found. "We just started picking up rocks," she later remembered, "and tried to decide which worms to deal with." Sullivan ordered an immediate 5 percent budget cut while Parks began life-or-death negotiations with federal lenders over the university's huge and long overdue construction debts.

At issue was the disposition of the $1.8 million that Swedish Hospital had offered in March for Marycrest Hall. Officials from the federal Department of Housing and Urban Development (HUD) demanded that the university turn over its million dollar equity from the sale to pay down its outstanding federal loans. Because this debt was subject to a partial moratorium and low interest rates, Parks was more worried about the $1.5 million due on the Ziegler notes in less than two years. She asked the federal agencies to permit the university to use the sale income to refinance all of its obligations, public and private. This was unprecedented, but Parks argued that the alternative would cripple the university. She knew that federal officials were not eager to foreclose on such white elephants as Campion Hall.

While these talks continued over the spring and summer, Sullivan forged ahead with new programs, including the university's first doctoral degree, in Educational Leadership, developed by dean Dr. John Morford. A federal grant of $140,000 permitted Dr. Edwin Weihe, Thomas Trebon and their colleagues to begin planning in earnest for Form II of the Matteo Ricci College, whose

Dr. Gary Zimmerman took over as dean of Science and Engineering and later succeeded Bill Guppy as academic vice president. Dean Eileen Ridgway and her successor Pat Ferris (far left) preside at one of the last "capping ceremonies" for graduating nurses.

Fr. William LeRoux, SJ, and Fr. James Powers, SJ, confer over plans for the new Matteo Ricci College.

first students were due in 1978. Sullivan also used the summer to organize his administration and he outlined an ambitious agenda to revamp financial management, personnel procedures, fund raising, intramural athletics, and student recruitment through, among other things, "development of a new market in the Bellevue area." To assist in accomplishing these goals, the trustees approved Sullivan's selection of Father Lemieux as Chancellor; and Father Jack Lawlor, SJ, became executive assistant to the president.

Above all, Sullivan pledged to revitalize the "general ethos of the university." In July 1976 he told the trustees, "The spirit of the university is a delicate element and cannot be neglected. Father Ryan's administration created a great expectation of change. It is my intention to maintain this momentum but to be realistic about the budget stresses and budget limitations." As part of this commitment, he launched discussions throughout campus to distill the university's first formal statement of its mission.

The 1976 school year opened with the happy news that enrollment had grown to 3,507, fueled chiefly by expanding graduate programs

which compensated for an almost 6 percent decline in undergraduate registrations. The following spring, John Eshelman succeeded Gerald Cleveland as dean of the Albers School of Business, and Pat Ferris took over the School of Nursing from Eileen Ridgway, who had been trying to retire for the past year.

The university continued digging itself "out of the deepest hole," in Dr. Parks' phrase, created by years of deficit spending. On April 22, 1977, Father Sullivan informed the trustees that HUD had accepted Seattle University's plan for Marycrest sale proceeds. Thanks to Parks' negotiating skills and the intercession of former Governor Dan Evans with HUD Secretary Carla Hills, the university had retained equity of some $500,000 which it used to refinance the Ziegler debt through Pacific National Bank (now First Interstate).

The university was no longer staring potential bankruptcy in the face and it marked a personal triumph for Sullivan's leadership. But instead of receiving applause at the April 22 Board meeting, Sullivan found his presidency under direct attack from Father James Powers, a trus-

tee and dean of Arts and Sciences. The pretext, if not cause for Powers' challenge, was Sullivan's decision not to renew Father Mick Larkin, SJ, as vice president for students. Larkin was something of a protege of Powers, who had convinced Father Ryan to dismiss Father Cronin and name Larkin instead. Powers now blasted Sullivan's "prejudicial decision to terminate" Larkin and offered his own resignation as dean with the clear implication that the trustees had to choose between him and Sullivan.

Powers' play failed. Chairman O'Brien expressed the view that Sullivan was "doing a good job as president, but there could be a question about how he does some things." Sullivan freely confessed his own need "to narrow his separation from the university community as people," but the trustees did not regard this as a mortal sin. The motion was made for a "vote of support and commendation" for Sullivan. Sensing his defeat, Powers joined the other trustees in adopting it unanimously.

Powers resigned as dean but he made his complaint public by rapping Sullivan's "administrative style" in the *Spectator* a week later. Sullivan responded by holding an open forum to correct his admitted shortcomings "in terms of process and consultation." It was a trying but ultimately therapeutic time, and Sullivan's spirits were buoyed when his old friends at Seminex awarded him an honorary doctorate. Sullivan's new friends at Seattle University also stood by him.

The university became embroiled in a flap of another kind in the summer of 1977 when Sullivan moved to assert closer control over Connolly Center, which was deteriorating rapidly thanks to poorly supervised public use. Dr. Ken Nielsen, the new vice president for student life, reviewed the original federal documents governing the Center and discovered that the HEW loan in fact "restricts use of the building to instruction in physical education," notwithstanding Fitterer's pledges for community use. Sullivan wanted to intensify campus use of the facility to expand intramural sports, and angry residents organized the ''Central Area Parks Action Committee'' to oppose restrictions on non-student access. Sullivan responded by increasing public programming through the Boys Club, but hard feelings were left which would flare up and complicate later university relations with the city government.

Things were brighter on the financial front as the fall of 1977 approached. Kip Toner, Sullivan's new director of student financial aid (and later business manager), offered a concrete demonstration of how higher productivity could be accomplished without sacrificing quality. By aggressively pursuing federal aid and compensation for work-study, he allowed Sullivan to cut the allocation of tuition income for student aid from $800,000 to $550,000 without any net reduction in benefits. Cost-cutting did claim one victim, however, when the ASSU closed the books on the *Aegis* (it has since been revived in an abbreviated form).

Thanks in large part to the work of Chancellor Lemieux, the university's endowment had passed the $7 million mark by September. The sale of a parcel of Westlake Mall property donated by the Henry Broderick estate and Gund Foundation yielded half a million dollars, and restaurateur Ivar Haglund donated a Queen Anne Hill apartment building which was later sold for $300,000.

To systematize ''deferred giving,'' Sullivan began work to establish the Seattle University Foundation for soliciting and managing bequests. ''Deferred maintenance'' was also very much on the trustees' minds in 1977. As the university's fiscal health improved, its physical state continued to decline as years of inadequate upkeep took their toll. An architectural and engineering survey of campus buildings was conducted which, among other things, revealed that the Teatro Inigo was on the verge of collapse. Soon after, demolition crews brought down the house.

The university continued to rebuild as enrollment increased to 3,639 that fall. The most gratifying figures of all came in October 1977 when the university audit revealed a budget surplus of $98,275 for the preceding fiscal year. The sight of black ink on the university's books was a novelty, but not unprecedented. The difference in this case was that the university's debt and its current spending were both under control for the first time in a decade.

This tiny surplus, not even 1 percent of the budget, was no accident or anomaly; it was the first symptom of genuine financial recovery after a long illness. As Father Sullivan later described it, ''It was the biggest hundred thousand dollars I'll ever see.''

Performance on the basketball court was another matter as the Chieftains finished another disappointing season. Jack Schalow was tapped to replace Bill O'Connor as coach in March 1978. That same month, Father LeRoux's interim succession of Powers as dean of Arts and Sciences was formally approved. In May, the campus was stunned when a local radio station revealed that the university's director of gifts, Archille Bourque, was moonlighting by selling diplomas and transcripts from a fictitious ''Pacific Northwest University.'' Sullivan promptly dismissed Bourque lest the scandal reflect on the real university. It didn't, and improving finances permitted the administration to begin to lift faculty salaries. The trustees also authorized a master's degree in transportation engineering and the purchase of a new computer. Before year's end, the university began negotiations to buy the Johnson & Sons Mortuary on Madison Street.

Over 3,600 students, including the first products of Matteo Ricci College's Form I program, arrived on campus in the fall of 1978. Sullivan was able to report on many new developments—all of them positive. During the preceding summer, the university's budget had registered a

Business Dean John Eshelman secured accreditation for the university MBA program and later became Provost.

The Dalai Lama's visit in October 1979 signalled the university's return to the international arena.

record operating surplus of $620,000. This windfall was allocated to catching up with maintenance, creating a faculty development fund, and reducing the university's long-term debt.

Fr. Greg Lucey, SJ, became provost and joked, "Wherever I went, Bill [Sullivan] always seemed to be in command."

Also during the summer, Genevieve Albers advocated and offered to fund a program to bring top business and financial experts to lecture on campus each year, which became the Albers Business Forum. At the same time, a group of area business leaders raised almost $600,000 to give the university its first endowed professorial chair, in memory of Thomas F. Gleed, a former president of Seafirst Bank and a university benefactor.

The university also made some headway in its effort to acquire the Pacific School site for an intramural field. This ambition had taken a bizarre turn in 1976 when, without public notice or discussion, the US Postal Service bought the property for a mail handling center. The university's protests were ignored so it filed suit to compel the government to prepare an environmental impact statement before proceeding with construction. The courts agreed, and enjoined development of the site in July 1978. In this game, a stalemate was an advantage for the university, but there were many more moves yet to be made.

That same month, the board of trustees approved Sullivan's proposal to redesignate the vacant provost position as a vice presidency for planning. Sullivan already had a candidate in mind, Father Greg Lucey, SJ, a fellow native of Prairie du Chien, Wisconsin. As in most small towns, the families of Prairie du Chien were all well acquainted — among them, the Sullivans, Burtons (Sullivan's mother's family) and the Luceys. When Lucey entered the town's Jesuit high school, Campion, as a freshman, Sullivan was a senior and captain of Lucey's cadet unit. As Lucey later joked, "Wherever I went, Bill always seemed to be in command." When Lucey became rector of Campion, Sullivan was on his

board of trustees. When the school was closed, Lucey followed Sullivan's advice and took his doctorate in educational administration.

Now Sullivan wanted him in Seattle as his right-hand man. Lucey recalled, "There was a certain excitement about what [Sullivan] was trying to achieve there, about his hopes for the place." He agreed to join Sullivan's administration in September.

The most significant milestone of 1978 was completion of the university's new mission statement, which Sullivan presented at the beginning of the school year. The document committed the institution to three fundamental purposes: teaching, helping students grow as persons, and preparing them for service to society. In his address to the faculty-staff convocation, Father Sullivan elaborated on the statement by reminding his audience, "If we are truly going to be the kind of university that we express in our mission statement, we have to say to ourselves, every person in this university is a teacher." Sullivan stressed that this shared responsibility extended to helping students grow as individuals and to instilling in them a sense of obligation to their society. "There is no possible way that we can hope that these young men and women five and ten and fifteen years down the road will truly be serving society unless they can find in us, their teachers, the staff and the administration, a real sense of service."

Students *could* find just such a sense of service on campus, and above all in veteran Jesuits such as Fathers Lemieux, Cowgill and Earl. The example of their lives only magnified the shock when all three died within 48 hours of each other early in January 1979. Despite a bitter winter storm on January 15, St. James Cathedral overflowed with mourners for the three Jesuit heroes. Father Sullivan eulogized Seattle University's beloved chancellor and two selfless colleagues. Each had earned the epitaph, *Si monumentum requiris, circumspice* — If you seek his monument, look around.

Trustee Gene Lynn funded conversion of a defunct mortuary into a new home for the School of Nursing and his Careage Corporation later built the Bessie Burton Skilled Nursing Residence.

The physical renewal of the university took a significant step forward in February 1979 when the Murdock Foundation offered a $150,000 matching grant for the purchase of the Johnson & Sons Mortuary. Trustee Gene Lynn, president of the Careage Corporation, which develops and operates nursing centers, came forward to meet this challenge. He offered to rehabilitate the building at cost as a new home for the nursing school. This was the first significant campus development project in a decade. Transforming a mortuary into a home for the nursing school symbolized the victory of life over death in more ways than one, and a grateful board named the building for Gene Lynn.

The university inched closer to another goal when the Postal Service abandoned its plans for the Pacific School site. The bureaucrats ran up the white flag after Senator Warren Magnuson threatened to hold up their entire budget unless they started negotiating with the university. The Postal Service grudgingly complied but rejected an offer of $560,000 in July 1979.

Progress continued on the financial front as the university snapped up the Alcoa Building at Broadway and Madison for $1 million borrowed from the Albers trust. The property was sold five years later for almost two and a half times as much. Meanwhile, other investments and

gifts raised the endowment past $8 million. The trustees welcomed Genevieve Albers as a member in April, and Father Powers quietly took his leave from the board and, eventually, the campus.

July 1979 marked another financial milestone for the university's budget. Dr. Parks informed the trustees that "for the first time in history we did not have to borrow from the bank on June 30."

"Bridge loans" were used routinely to pay bills while the university waited for its cash flow to catch up (something it had not always done, which created the operating deficit). Now the university carried enough money forward in its accounts to meet operating expenses without the bank's help.

Improving finances also permitted the university to continue to upgrade salaries. The board approved a 13-percent average raise for the fiscal year ending in June 1980. This was not fast enough for some who revived a drive for collective bargaining. This in turn sparked a rancorous dispute over the labor status of Jesuits on the faculty, who, ironically, had voted on both sides of the previous union petition in 1972. The issue was rendered moot by a case involving unionization at Yeshiva University in New York. The federal courts decided that all faculty

members were involved too deeply in management to claim conventional bargaining rights as workers.

The 1979/80 school year marked another increase in enrollment, which reached 4,150, only a few dozen registrations short of the university's all time record set in 1965. Among the new students were over 200 Matteo Ricci Form I graduates. These young men and women scored so well as a group in national aptitude tests that amazed evaluators came out personally to verify the results.

The news that the university had passed its accreditation review with flying colors in the fall of 1979 offered a convenient moment for William Guppy to relinquish his seat as academic vice president and return to the classroom. During his nine years of leadership, Guppy had helped strengthen and broaden the university's academic program by introducing new bachelor's degrees in criminal justice and police science, humanities, social science, and a variety of medical technologies and health specialties, as well as master's degrees in a host of disciplines and its first doctorate in educational leadership. Not coincidentally, enrollment had recovered from a nadir of barely 2,900 students.

The new master's degree in software engineering provided an example of the univer-

Women Chieftains April Lewallen, Debbie Henderson and All-American Sue Turina (far right) achieved new heights. Meanwhile, the Chieftain men experienced new lows, as registered in Fr. Sullivan's expression during a loss to the U of W.

sity's ability to innovate despite financial adversity. The opportunity for the program was created a few years earlier when the university replaced its ancient computer with modern data processing technology. It then occurred to Father Frank Wood that there might be some interest in software design courses which went beyond the rudimentary programming courses already available. Wood pursued the idea with Orville Dunn, his frequent collaborator at Boeing Computer Services, and Dunn assigned Larry Peters from his staff to help Wood craft the new curriculum. Father Wood recruited Kyu Lee to launch the program, and three years later the university awarded its first master's degrees in software engineering and later extended instruction to undergraduates, making it one of the leading schools in the field. The university had identified a need in the community and moved to fill it.

There were other needs to be filled. After so many years of preoccupation with internal problems, Father Sullivan knew it was time for the president of Seattle University to reach out to the community not merely to ask for its help but to offer service and leadership in return. In this undertaking, Sullivan proved energetic and effective. Since taking office only three years earlier, he had already been elected to the governing boards of the International Federation of Catholic Universities and the American Council on Education, and helped found the Washington Student Loan Guaranty Association to expand student aid. Sullivan also set an example of local service by joining the boards of United Way of King County and the Greater Seattle Chamber of Commerce.

The university returned to the international arena in October 1979 when it hosted the Dalai Lama and conferred an honorary doctorate on the exiled leader of Tibet's Buddhists. The Dalai Lama blessed a scarf for Pope Paul II, which Father Sullivan delivered into the pontiff's hands a few days later in Washington, D.C.

Fall brought more staff changes when Gary Zimmerman succeeded Bill Guppy as academic vice president and Marylou Wyse became dean of the Graduate School. Meanwhile Father Lucey and Dr. George Pierce worked to refine and implement a new five year plan to guide the university's academic and physical development. In October 1979, the Postal Service finally relented and accepted the university's offer of $978,000 for the Pacific School site. The next month, Cornell C. Maier, president of Kaiser Aluminum, arrived on campus to launch the first Albers Business Forum.

As 1980 began, the university found its attention, like that of the entire world, seized by the hostage crisis in Tehran. The issue was not abstract on a campus that included 69 Iranian nationals, the largest nationality out of 415 foreign-born students, and the administration moved to ensure the safety of its Iranian students.

That spring, the university decided the fate of its collection of ancient apartment buildings. The former Bellarmine Apartments (later dubbed McCusker Hall) near Loyola were demolished, but trustees decided to spare the 1898-vintage Casarucia Apartments, now Marian Hall, for three more years. The building survived nearly three times that long.

In March 1980, the trustees decided at Father Sullivan's suggestion to take a hard look at the future of intercollegiate athletics. The glory days were definitely behind the Chieftains, although female hoopsters such as Sue Turina, who scored 1,600 points between 1978 and '81, were doing their best to preserve the university's reputation. The intercollegiate program was running almost $300,000 in the red, and athletic director Eddie O'Brien told the administration he really needed a budget of at least $1 million to field credible teams.

The task of evaluating the athletic program and exploring alternatives was given to Father Lucey, who assembled a panel of members of the university community for the review. Between February and the end of the March, this task force conducted scores of interviews and commissioned a telephone poll of students, alumni, officials, faculty members, and Chieftain fans of every stripe. Speculation about what the task force might recommend was rampant on campus, prompting the April Fool's Day edition of the *Spectator* to announce that the university would "drop academics."

The task force's final report on March 31, 1980, was not quite that dramatic, but it did propose that the university withdraw from NCAA Division I competition and limit itself to NAIA play among local small colleges. It also supported expanding intramural teams and "life sports," i.e., the kinds of physical activities students were likely to pursue beyond college. Such a program had the added benefit of making it much easier to meet federal regulations for parity between athletic opportunities for men and women.

The task force used the university's mission statement as its touchstone in evaluating alternative athletic programs, but it was not blind to the political sensitivities involved. In arriving at this plan, the report found that less than a third of students or alumni supported the current level of competition. Only the loyal members of the Tomahawk Club protested axing Division I play. Although implementation of the task force's recommendations offered more than $300,000 in annual savings, finances were not as significant a factor as some suspected in the trustees' decision to accept the report. The question was framed in terms of competing academic priorities. Faced with choosing among student aid, program development, salary increases, or a competitive Division I effort, the board sacrificed the latter.

Some disgruntled fans hung an effigy of Sullivan on campus, but the *Spectator* praised the decision (and a year later, the Alumni Association, fully cognizant of the simmering contro-

versy, honored Sullivan for "courageous and creative leadership"). Eddie O'Brien resigned in protest, and was succeeded by Dr. Richard McDuffie, while Dr. Nielsen chaired a new Sports Transition Committee to plan the details of the new program.

The June 1980 commencement featured the first Matteo Ricci graduates, and enrollment the following September set a new record at 4,380 students. The university also accomplished a long-standing goal when its master's degree in business administration received full accreditation. That same September, David Kurtz was named the first Thomas Gleed professor, and the university celebrated the golden jubilee of Father McGoldrick, who remained an active force in campus life and a living link between the university's past and future.

As one sports era ended, a new one began with the official opening of the Intramural Field in October 1980. Senator Magnuson, whose influence on the Postal Service had made the field possible, presided as he had at so many other campus dedications. It turned out to be the last hurrah for one of the university's best friends; the Senator lost his bid for re-election the following month.

In January 1981, the Chieftain men suffered one last humiliation in their final Division I season when it was discovered that several members of the basketball squad were not academically eligible under intercollegiate rules. Coach Schalow departed for what became a successful career in professional basketball while Tom Schneeman took over the demoralized Chieftains for the rest of the season. He was succeeded by Len Nadone in May.

On the positive side, Gene Lynn's Careage Corporation created a $1 million endowment for rural nursing in March, which helped to increase the university's total endowment to more than $11 million by the following May. The fiscal year ended in June with a positive balance of $775,000, and during its summer retreat, the trustees set

Senator Magnuson presides over the dedication of the new Intramural Field, his last hurrah on behalf of the university.

long-range goals for increasing student aid, enhancing faculty salaries and quality, developing campus facilities, and expanding educational resources. But how would the university pay for these ambitions?

Raising tuition to $95 per credit hour was part of the answer. The university had shifted to a credit-hour accounting system to monitor costs more closely. The system helped in keeping pace with the high rate of inflation, and administrators were relieved that rising tuition did not dampen enrollment. Another record was set in the fall of 1981 as 4,633 students crowded onto campus. The school year began with more personnel changes as Gary Zimmerman became executive vice president with the charge of improving "academic efficiency" by 20 percent over the coming four years, and Mary Lou Wyse moved into the academic vice president's chair temporarily (Thomas Longin was named to the position the following April).

Father Sullivan provided the other part of the financial answer at the fall convocation when he told the assembled staff and faculty, "The message that I communicate to you this morning is very simply this: I am profoundly convinced that we must at this time launch a major funds campaign, that we must tell our story to this community." Sullivan added, "It is a startling fact that in its 90th year, this university has never launched a comprehensive major funds campaign in this community."

Correcting that omission had already begun under the direction of Father Lucey, who had succeeded James Lyddy as vice president for university relations the previous December. While Dr. Pierce and his staff drafted plans for the university's physical and academic development, Lucey began, in his words, to "cultivate major giving on a regular basis" by, for example, reviving the President's Club for donors who gave $1,000 or more annually.

The foremost barrier to serious fund raising, Lucey discovered, was the university's own timidity. "Expectations were that people would not give, so they made only modest requests," he explained, and many on campus "were fairly cautious about dreaming." Father Sullivan was not among them, but he was suitably cautious about raising hopes that could not be fulfilled. Fund raising consultants advised that no campaign should be announced until at least half of its stated goal had been lined up in advance. Thus, the "Capital Campaign" really began two years before it was announced publicly in 1983.

In the fall of 1981 Sister Rosaleen Trainor, CSJP, was named the first McGoldrick Teaching Fellow, a fitting tribute to the man who had introduced Jesuit co-education half a century earlier. Also that fall, Hildegard Hendrickson was named the university's first professor of banking, a position subsidized by Rainier Bank. The university's second endowed professorial chair was established in the humanities by Mrs. Theiline Pigott McCone (Paul Pigott's widow, who had married John McCone, director of the Central Intelligence Agency in the Kennedy Administration). Other benefactors would later endow chairs in honor of Robert O'Brien and Father Gaffney.

As 1982 began, the drive for more "productivity" in the classroom began to produce new strains. A decision to put the Fine Arts department on "probation" sparked angry protests before it was rescinded. The denial of tenure to more than one faculty member and layoffs produced lawsuits and civil rights complaints — all decided in the university's favor. The pain of these austerity moves was redeemed in July, however, when the university was able to use its cash surplus to pay off the last $640,000 of debt remaining from the Ziegler notes.

The vestiges of a troubled past were finally being laid to rest, but so too were some of the university's greatest builders. Father Carmody died on July 26, 1982, and Father McNulty followed November 25. Father McGoldrick, however, seemed to be immortal. He was on hand

when the university established a special scholarship program for future community leaders, endowed by a bequest from Sue M. Naef. Then, on April 26, 1983, the last of the Four Horsemen of Loyola fell as he had lived, at full gallop.

Mrs. Theiline Pigott McCone (left) continued the Pigott family tradition of university service. Sister Rosaleen Trainor, CSJP, became the first McGoldrick Teaching Fellow in 1981, honoring the man who pioneered Jesuit co-education half a century before. Dr. George Pierce (below) looks over a model of the campus before its transformation into a "University Park."

Overleaf: The university community gathers in the Quadrangle to launch its centennial celebration on October 5, 1990.

Inset: Seattle City Councilmember Sam Smith and St. Michelle Winery executive Kerry Godes are two outstanding alumni.

THE MISSION RENEWED

Enrollment during 1982/1983 school year declined, albeit slightly, for the first time in a decade. The reason was simple: the supply of American teenagers was running low as the post-war generation entered its twenties and "thirty-something" years. But the baby boom still reverberated on campus as older students pursued advanced degrees and working professionals returned to upgrade their resumes.

A study of 1982 registrations revealed that over 60 percent of the Seattle University students were 23 years of age or older; in 1968 this group had represented less than 32 percent of the student body. While Angel Petrich garnered new distinction for university women by winning All-American basketball honors as a Chieftain, a study of the 1983 enrollment also revealed that women now constituted a majority of the student population of 4,544.

The same study showed that the university enjoyed the second highest minority enrollment of any four-year institution in the Northwest — major progress since the stormy days of May 1970. A new scholarship for African-American high school students was later established to help maintain the momentum. The Institute of Public Service was shifted to the Albers School of Business and a fourth year was added to Seattle Prep to accommodate those students who chose a more conventional path for their higher education.

Early in 1983, the university entertained an unexpected proposal from the president of the Cornish Institute for Arts, which was facing a crisis not unlike that weathered by the university in the previous decade. He suggested that Seattle University might assimilate Cornish and turn its Art Deco home on Capitol Hill into a satellite campus. The university's trustees were intrigued despite an estimated cost as high as $900,000 over the first three years of such an arrangement, but Cornish ultimately decided to save itself.

The Cornish discussion was a sidelight to the university's central focus on a visionary master plan to transform its campus into a "University Park," or as Dr. Pierce described it, "an emerald university in the heart of an emerald city." The first phase called for construction of a new Science and Engineering Building, which was originally sited on the parking lot east of the Pigott Building. The budget for the new building and other physical modernization was set at $8

million. The trustees added $3 million to endow student scholarships, almost $6 million to develop the university's academic "Margin of Excellence," and sundry projects, to arrive at a set of needs totaling $20 million. This was the goal established by the trustees when they decided in July to take the plunge with a public Capital Campaign.

Would the community respond? Would individuals, corporations and foundations really dig into their pockets during a recession and turn over $20 million to a little Jesuit college in the Central Area? What would they receive in return for such an investment? Father Sullivan delivered the answer during the fall 1983 convocation when he outlined the social challenges facing the university. He cited three key trends, beginning with the fragmentation of America's traditional "melting pot society" as minorities, women and others raised "strong voices for recognizing the distinctiveness of such groups and also for recognizing their right to be distinctive." Sullivan believed that this trend toward "cultural diversity is something we as a university have the opportunity and the challenge to live with and work with."

He found the second trend less sanguine, namely the "extraordinary expansion of the electronic dimensions of society." The rise of computers, video and instantaneous data transmission, Sullivan explained, had burst "the information float," which sustained the traditional

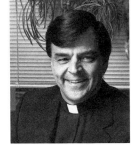

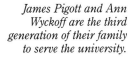

As the new assistant to the president for "Jesuit Identity,." Fr. John Topel, SJ, promotes "colleagueship" between lay and clerical members of the faculty.

James Pigott and Ann Wyckoff are the third generation of their family to serve the university.

university's power as an "information broker." The march of technology also promoted "a culture built on quantification," and it posed a crucial question: "Will the future definitions of knowledge be controlled by the computer [model] as either a switch on or a switch off, either a zero or a one? Is that to become the controlling epistemological fact in our culture?" If so, this putative progress sounded "a note of caution for people who are dedicated to a humanistic vision of education."

Finally, Sullivan cited the rise of "self-centeredness" as a "20th century kind of a solipsism" which contrasted with Catholic humanism's emphasis on community and fulfillment through service. In facing these trends, which threatened the atomization of culture, knowledge and individual identity, Sullivan saw the university as a laboratory and forum for the "debate on the nature of the human person." Sullivan closed his convocation address by challenging his listeners "to be alert, to be perceptive, and to be responsive, and I feel that we can do that by mining more deeply and refining more carefully the tradition of Christian humanism in which this university stands." Thus, Father Sullivan translated the generalities of the university's mission into a concrete struggle for humanistic values in shaping society's future. Here was a clarion battle cry for the Capital Campaign.

And who better to lead the charge than a new generation of the Pigott family? As 1983 drew to a close, Father Sullivan introduced James Pigott as the chair of the Capital Campaign. Jim was joined by his sister Ann Wyckoff, who chaired the President's Club, in renewing the great tradition of Pigott philanthropy begun by their grandfather William and continued by their parents Paul and Theiline.

The Capital Campaign began with much of its goal already pledged or banked, and its momentum never slowed thanks to the efforts of a large and enthusiastic steering committee. The sales pitch, Pigott recalls, was the obvious fact that Seattle University was becoming "an increasingly valuable civic asset," and echoing Sullivan's thesis, the appeal of the institution's "ethics and morality permeated the whole campaign."

Jim Pigott later explained to Father Lucey that the secret of successful fund raising was not to ask people to give until it hurt, "but until it felt really good." Among those feeling especially good were the Boeing Company, which helped to launch the campaign with $1 million, and Thomas Bannan, who contributed the last $2.5 million needed to finish the Science and Engineering Center that now bears his name.

More financial help became available late in 1983 when the new state Higher Education Facilities Authority was established. This gave Seattle University the opportunity to fund capital projects with tax-exempt bonds for the first time in its history. Meanwhile, the university expanded its real estate holdings, buying several small lots east of 12th Avenue and the REI Building on Madison. By the close of 1984, a $250,000 gift from the Northwest Foundation raised the Capital Campaign total to $15 million, three-fourths of the way toward its goal. The progress was so encouraging that Father Sullivan asked the trustees to accelerate the capital plan and give the green light to construction of a new Liberal Arts Faculty Building.

Fund raising was not the only activity during 1984 as Jeremy Stringer took over as vice president for student life and began revitalizing campus service programs. Sullivan and Dr. Stanford started working with the Archdiocese to develop a new Institute of Theological Studies, absorbing the old Corpus and SUMORE programs and expanding religious training on campus, and the faculty commenced a fresh review of the Core Curriculum.

Despite the small but worrisome decline in enrollment during the previous three years, the graduating class topped 1,000 for the first time in university history in June 1985, and total endowments neared $30 million. Also that summer, the Careage Corporation approached the university about converting Campion Hall into a nursing home; this idea never materialized but it planted seeds that would blossom five years later.

On May 2, 1986, one day shy of the 10th anniversary of Father Sullivan's presidency, ground was broken for the new Bannan Engineering and Science Building and the Liberal Arts Faculty Building. This occasion marked the first new construction undertaken by the university since work began on the Connolly Center 18 years earlier. Plans were also approved for a $1 million remodeling of the University Services Building and bookstore.

That same spring, Father Sullivan accepted the chairmanship of the Seattle Organizing Committee responsible for hosting the 1990 Goodwill Games. This latest act of leadership was only a step in a continuum. Father Sullivan's work in behalf of religious and social harmony had already been rewarded with special honors from the state chapter of the National Council of Christians and Jews in 1981 and the Anti-Defamation League of B'nai B'rith in 1983. He carried this work into international affairs by helping organize the 1983 Target Seattle effort to improve people-to-people communication between the United States and Soviet Union. Thus, Sullivan was well prepared for his new responsibilities as an impresario of international cooperation.

Athletics closer to home demanded Sullivan's attention as the 1986/87 school year began. The report of the Sports Review Task Force showed that the number of intramural teams had multiplied from 11 to 191 in the five years since reorganization of athletics. Intercollegiate performance, however, had sunk to a dismal 41 wins out of a total of 163 games in the latest academic year. As Sullivan later comment-

ed, "I know defeat is supposed to build character, but this was ridiculous." The trustees agreed and added scholarship funds and other resources to rebuild the intercollegiate program.

Father Sullivan also chose the fall of 1986 to renew his personal commitment to the university by pledging to continue as its president "at least though our centenary in 1991." Two key members of his team decided to pursue other interests. Gary Zimmerman left campus (he now directs the Seattle campus of Antioch College), and business dean John Eshelman took his seat as executive vice president. Dr. Virginia Parks returned to the classroom and handed her ledgers over to Denis Ransmeier — but not before erasing the last of $3.4 million in operating debt she had inherited in 1975.

By the end of 1986, the Capital Campaign had met and exceeded its goal by raising almost $26 million. Part of this success can be attributed to the extraordinary generosity of Marguerite Casey who ultimately contributed $4.5 million toward the completion of the Liberal Arts Faculty Building now named in her honor.

The university unveiled a new core curriculum for the 1987/88 school year, completing a four-year effort involving some 100 members of the administration and faculty under the direction of Father David Leigh, SJ. In seeking to immerse every undergraduate in the Jesuit tradition of liberal arts, the university constructed the new core in three phases: the foundations of wisdom, the person in society, and responsibility and service.

In the new core, each student progresses from a mastery of writing and the essentials of philosophy, the liberal arts and physical science, through psychology and the social sciences, into a deeper ethical examination, culminating in an interdisciplinary "senior synthesis" to apply the student's new understanding to a problem within his or her major. The approach reflects some of the insights gained in development of the Matteo Ricci College, but its roots go back much farther

Fr. Sullivan personally invited George Tsutakawa to create the Centennial Fountain as a new centerpiece and symbol for the university.

Marian Hall stood for 90 years before it was demolished in 1988 for the new Quadrangle.

The new Bannan Center begins to rise in 1986.

in time. As Father John Topel, SJ, Assistant to the President for Jesuit Identity, wrote in the preamble to the new core —

A Jesuit liberal arts education assumes that you will become what you desire. All the courses [in the core] aim at helping you clarify, broaden and deepen your most important question in life: "What do you REALLY want?" When that question is deepened, most of us discover that what we really want is the knowledge, skills and power to build a world of justice and love.

The university was no longer afraid to become what it desired, thanks to the spectacular reception its appeals received in the community. Even as the new Bannan and Casey Buildings were dedicated in the fall of 1987, Father Lucey was already exploring a new "Centennial Campaign" while Dr. George Pierce initiated a new cycle of strategic planning to guide the university into its second century. Construction priority was given to a quadrangle plaza, and Father Sullivan approached George Tsutakawa about designing a fountain as its centerpiece. Development of a "Life Sciences Building" south of Loyola Hall was approved before year's end, and Gene Lynn again raised the possibility of constructing a "Convalescent Center" on campus.

This momentum ran into a bureaucratic brick wall when the City's Department of Construction and Land Use (DCLU) raised, in Sullivan's word, "astonishing" objections to the university's master plan. The crux of the dispute was the university's eastward expansion, including acquisition and development of the City-owned "bus barn" block on 14th Avenue. Fulfilling these ambitions depended on DCLU's approval of zoning changes to allow institutional use of lots currently occupied by small businesses and homes. This rekindled neighborhood suspicions left over from controversies about public use of the Connolly Center.

Despite five years of planning and negotia-

tion between the university and City officials, DCLU unexpectedly took a stand in early 1988 which prevented development of two-thirds of this expansion. Dr. Pierce decried the City's objections as "extremely frustrating and disappointing and some may even be illegal." The trustees vowed to fight all the way to the City Council, which had the final say on the needed zoning amendments.

The spring of 1988 was a time of transition as Mary Malarkey succeeded Father Lucey as vice president for university relations. After a decade of administration and fund raising, Lucey had decided to renew his spiritual life as a priest and he now serves as rector of the Jesuit community at Marquette University. Robert O'Brien also decided it was time to step down as chairman of the board of trustees, having helped lead the university through some of its darkest nights and brightest days. O'Brien turned his gavel over to Jim Pigott on July 25, 1988, but remains a trustee.

The university was changing physically as Marian Hall fell in May to make way for the new quadrangle. By then the Bannan Center was being occupied under the guidance of Science and Engineering dean Terry J. van der Werff. The building became home to the Engineering Design Center, an innovation begun in 1987 to give engineering students hands-on experience in solving design problems for local industry.

The trustees decided to locate the proposed Biology Center in an underground grotto adjacent to Bannan and approved a new $16.5 million capital budget. This new plan will be implemented commencing 1991, and calls for new landscaping to define the campus perimeter as a welcoming gateway, not a wall between the university and its neighborhood.

Another project scheduled to begin in 1991 is the remodeling of the Madison Building. This former cable car barn and original site of the School of Engineering is to be transformed into a new home of the fine arts department, for

which Father Hayden Vachon had collected all those dimes and nickels. His "eke box" had been tapped to help make ends meet during the university's darkest days, but this special fund— which totals $300,000 including all "lost" interest — has been restored at Father Sullivan's direction. At last, it will be spent according to Father Vachon's wishes.

The 1988/89 school year began with welcome news as enrollment rebounded to 4,416. Father Sullivan reported to the trustees, "After three years of declining enrollment and credit hours, we seem to have turned the corner." The administration also set about addressing the trustee's priority on increasing minority enrollment, which had slipped by 20 percent in recent years.

On February 27, 1989, the Seattle City council approved a modified campus master plan. The City later agreed to an elaborate land swap which gave the university the old bus barn site for a new intramural field. During the spring and summer of 1989, the trustees committed to a three-year plan for significantly improving faculty salaries. They also agreed to phase out undergraduate study at the School of Education and substitute an array of master's degree programs to meet the more demanding standards facing modern teachers. Meanwhile, Father Sullivan reorganized his administration that summer, combining the executive and academic vice presidency into a restored provost position to which John Eshelman was named.

The university's accreditation was renewed in 1989 and the evaluation team praised the restoration of financial stability under Sullivan's leadership. Nevertheless, the accreditation report suggested a number of areas for improvement, including the library, compensation, fine arts facilities, and faculty and student participation in governance. Work had in fact already begun on most of these reforms.

In the fall of 1989, the university undertook its first serious experiment in satellite programs

Rosa Parks, who launched the modern civil rights movement by refusing to sit in the back of the bus, visited campus in May 1990. Former student Quincy Jones returned to accept an honorary doctorate in June.

by offering graduate education classes in Federal Way and master's degree in business administration courses in Bellevue. These innovations helped to pump enrollment to 4,514, notwithstanding an annual tuition of $9,990. More gratifying still, the university's minority enrollment rose to 519 from 420 a year earlier.

Despite these successes, the university felt a growing sense of concern about the future as it faced the gradual diminution of the ranks of Jesuits. With only modest overstatement, John Eshelman summed up the problem: "We used to have 90 Jesuits with an average age of 30. Now we have 30 Jesuits with an average age of 90." In the university's centennial year, active Jesuits constituted barely 10 percent of the faculty, and the foreseeable trend is that the Jesuit cadre on campus will continue to shrink in absolute as well as relative numbers. As a consequence, "We face the real danger of losing our philosophic and ethical bearings," according to Eshelman. In the words of James Stark, former acting dean of Arts and Sciences, "We must figure out how to remain a Jesuit university without a Jesuit presence."

The urgency of this touches all members of the university community, Catholic and non-Catholic alike, and a conscious campaign is now underway to promote "colleagueship" between lay persons and Jesuits. In Sister Rosaleen Trainor's view, the success or failure of this effort will depend on whether the "Jesuit ethos translates into a tradition people value" independent of its Jesuit custodians. She believes that this demands that every member of the university community ask the fundamental question, "What does it mean to serve faith and justice?" That is the question Ignatius had asked nearly half a millennium before, and it is the question upon which the entire university continues to reflect as it re-evaluates its mission statement. The most recent draft reads in part,

The educational mission of Seattle University for today and tomorrow grows out of a religious vision and out of the values that are inherent in that mission.... The most fundamental value of this vision is the nobility of the human person, understood as a free and intelligent being with a transcendent destiny....

The final educational goal for all our activities, our ultimate purpose, is the growth of our students as persons. We endeavor to assist our students to become knowledgeable, skilled, and confident; to experience liberation and integration; to grow in breadth of perspective and depth of concern; and to develop their spiritual and ethical talents.

This commitment was given artistic expression when George Tsutakawa's supple, flame-like Centennial fountain was unveiled in September 1989. The new biology complex opened the following January as a fitting introduction to the university's 99th year.

The approach of centennials usually generates loftier words than deeds, but Seattle University pursued a remarkable year of concrete progress and fulfillment, beginning with a redoubled effort to attract and serve minority

Vice President Dan Quayle visited to kick off the 1990 Goodwill Games. The Centennial Children's Literacy Project formed a living link with Seattle University's beginnings as a parish school and inner-city college.

students. In February 1990 Security Pacific Bank made a grant of $200,000 for minority scholarships, adding to the $75,000 it donated the year before.

In April, the university welcomed Rosa Parks, whose refusal to yield her bus seat to a white man in Montgomery, Alabama, in 1955 marked the beginning of the modern civil rights movement. She made the keynote address to representatives of 22 area colleges and universities attending the 1990 Northwest Minority Student Leadership Conference held on campus. This was followed in May by a major conference on cultural diversity, the Consultation on American Pluralism — A Northwest Perspective, co-sponsored by the university and the American Jewish Committee.

Also in May, Father Sullivan returned from the International Peace Climb in the Himalaya Mountains in time to reach another summit when he was named Seattle's "First Citizen" by the Seattle-King County Association of Realtors. Spring brought more successes as the demand of over 300 students compelled the university to expand its Eastside Education Center in Bellevue. Before the school year ended, Dr. Margaret

Haggerty was chosen to become the first woman dean of the School of Education, and Benes Aldana became the first Filipino elected president of the student body.

In June, internationally acclaimed composer, performer and producer Quincy Jones returned to campus after a 40 year absence to receive an honorary doctorate. With the 1990 commencement, the university's accumulated total number of graduates passed 30,000. That year's class had the added satisfaction of learning that they had earned their degrees at what *U.S. News and World Report* deemed to be one of the 10 best regional universities in the West.

The Goodwill Games drew fresh acclaim in July with world-class athletic competition, a triumphant arts festival, and serious conferences on trade, politics and culture. One of the most important — and passionate — of these exchanges took place on campus over the issues of human rights. Father Sullivan's leadership in hosting the Games was widely praised, and the skeptics (obviously unfamiliar with the university's own financial discipline under Sullivan's hand) were astounded when the Seattle Organizing Committee balanced its books.

July also marked the golden jubilees of three

Seattle University Jesuits, Fathers James Reichmann, William LeRoux, and Louis Sauvain. The university remembered that Jesuits still face great peril in the world, and the trustees approved an official commemoration of the November 16, 1989, murders of six Jesuit educators and their two lay assistants in El Salvador.

With the approach of the fall, the university turned its mind to a happier anniversary, its own centenary, but again deeds counted more than words as it organized the Centennial Children's Literacy Project. Under the direction of Sonja Griffin, this program now provides university volunteers to tutor Seattle school children in reading and writing.

In September, two pieces of good news arrived from Rome. First, on the 25th, Pope John Paul II issued a pronouncement on education *Ex Corde Ecclesiae* affirming that "The responsibility for maintaining and strengthening the Catholic identity of the university rests primarily with the university itself." This statement reversed a 1985 draft policy giving Church officials, not university administrators, custodianship for the religious fidelity of Catholic schools. Father Sullivan had joined other selected American Catholic educators in a critique of the original

Fr. Timothy Healy, SJ, director of the New York City Public Library and former president of Georgetown University, warned against "two dangers that beset the laborers at centennials."

policy and, it appeared, in earning a Papal vote of confidence.

This was followed on September 27 — the 450th anniversary of the founding of the Society of Jesus — with the installation of Father Stephen Sundborg, rector of Seattle University's Jesuit community, as head of the entire Oregon province. Sundborg took charge of 380 Jesuits in continuing the mission launched a century and a half earlier by Father Peter DeSmet in the Northwestern wilderness. Sundborg was succeeded as rector by Father Robert Grimm. At the same time, former trustee, rector and provincial Father Frank Case became an assistant to superior general Father Hans Peter Kolvenbach in Rome.

By this time, work was nearing completion on the Bessie Burton Sullivan Skilled Nursing Residence east of Campion Hall. The new convalescent care complex was named at Gene Lynn's insistence in honor of the mother of Fa-

ther Sullivan and Sister Kathleen Sullivan, RSCJ, who has been a member of the mathematics faculty since 1987. Built and operated for the university by Lynn's Careage Corporation, this facility ultimately will house 135 residents while providing a state-of-the-art learning environment for training nurses in gerontological care and other specialized disciplines. When the center opened late in 1990, Nazleh Vizatelli, dean of the Seattle University School of Nursing from 1944 to 1952, was one of its first residents, thereby completing a circle of service from teacher to student and student to teacher.

The year also marked the passing of more than one old friend: Father Gerard Evoy, the first vice president of university relations; Mrs. Theiline Pigott McCone, regent and generous benefactor; Gustave Stern, a long-time and much-loved music teacher; and William Woods, regent, trustee and one of the heroes of 1970 who helped to save the university in its hour of greatest financial need.

That crisis now seemed remote as the official celebration of Seattle University's centennial began in October 1990. The university was stronger than at any time in its history with a record enrollment of 4,640, an endowment of nearly $40 million, magnificent new buildings and public spaces, and a new capital campaign in preparation under the leadership of Puget Power chairman John Ellis.

And what a distance Seattle University had traveled in the century since Father Laure wrote his first glowing accounts of frontier Seattle and Father Van Gorp surveyed the overgrown hillside that would become a campus. How much Seattle had grown since Fathers Garrand and Sweere arrived to take charge of Father Prefontaine's "elephant" and introduce the city's young to the rigors and rewards of a Jesuit education.

Incredible changes had taken place in the century-long evolution from Immaculate Conception School, virtually a one-room schoolhouse serving the city's poorest parish — to Seattle College and its hodgepodge of surplus buildings bursting with war veterans and the first co-eds in Jesuit educational history — to Seattle University, the Northwest's largest independent center of higher learning and a great metropolitan university in the heart of the region's economic and cultural capital.

Any institution that had come so far, overcome such daunting obstacles, achieved such great heights, and faced a future so bright with promise could reasonably indulge in the sin of pride. But not Seattle University.

"There are two dangers that beset the laborers at centennials," warned Father Timothy Healy, SJ, former president of Georgetown University and now director of the New York City Public Library, as he sounded the keynote for Seattle University's celebration on October 5, 1990. "The first is the past itself. It is so easy to lose oneself in its intricacies, to wander with delight and gratitude through the minds and hearts of founding fathers, to admire their courage and vision, and thus to make the whole year-long enterprise an exercise in nostalgia."

Healy continued, "The other danger is in exactly the opposite direction, to take off in wild flights into the future.... The most sensible and profoundly useful thing that Seattle University can do this year is to treat both past and future with a wary eye and focus on the instant moment."

Steering this intellectual and spiritual course between past and future toward a reaffirmation of the values manifest in the institutional life of today was precisely the issue Father Sullivan put before the university community at the fall 1990 convocation —

What are the values that have animated our first hundred years? What are the values that must be kept alive in the decades ahead if we are to be this Seattle University?

I find myself focusing on our understanding

and appreciation of a certain vision of the human person. From the revelation, out of the centuries of philosophical and theological reflection, has come a vision of the human being as God's creation, as intelligent and free, as destined for the transcendent, as having inalienable rights and moral responsibilities.

Some elements of this vision have become part of the classical Western view of the human person. But some key elements are rejected — angrily, contemptuously, massively — by competing modern views of the human.

What was for the founders and builders of this university for most of its first century taken for granted with regard to the nature of the person can no longer be presumed. We must be clearer, more explicit, more self-conscious and reflective about such ideas as freedom, spirituality, morality, rights, equality.

We must be clear about our values with regard to the person, about their foundations. And we must work together to build that vision, that understanding of the person into our curriculum, our student development, our learning and teaching, our community. We must if we are to continue to be this Seattle University.

Father Sullivan closed his centennial remarks by recalling Matteo Ricci's dying words to those who would succeed him. As a new generation inherits the legacy of Garrand, Sweere, McGoldrick, Corkery, Small, Lemieux, Gaffney, Sullivan, and all the men and women who built, taught, learned, served and sacrificed to create and sustain Seattle University for its first century, Ricci's challenge passes on both a heavy responsibility and an exhilarating mission for the work to come:

It will not be done without great effort and many perils, but I leave you standing before a door open to great accomplishments.

Fr. Sullivan challenged the university community to rededicate itself to "a vision of the human being as God's creation, as intelligent and free, as destined for the transcendent, as having inalienable rights and moral responsibilities."

HONOR ROLL OF
UNIVERSITY SERVICE:

*The following members of the faculty and staff each performed 20 or
more years of service in creating Seattle University.
(Honorifics and academic titles have been deleted.)*

Clarence Abello
Walter Aklin
Engelbert Axer, SJ
Mary Bartholet
Gerald Beezer, SJ
Ernest Bertini, SJ
Roger Blanchette, SJ
Dorothy Blystad
Hamida Bosmajian
Patrick Burke
Jean Bushman
Gerard Bussy, SJ
Carol Byrd
Walter Carmody
Robert Carmody, SJ
Ben Cashman
Chu Chiu Chang
Louis Christensen
Janet Claypool
Mary Cobelens
William Codd, SJ
James Connors, SJ
Vincent Conway, SJ
Paul Cook
John Corrigan, SJ
James Cowgill, SJ
Thomas Cunningham
Nickolas Damascus
Margaret Davies
Rose DeGracia
Khalil Dibee
Anna Dillon
Joseph Donovan, SJ
William Dore Jr.
Arthur Earl, SJ
Robert Egan. SJ
John Eshelman
Ann Fernandez
Patricia Ferris
Lewis Filler
Alice Fisher

Edward Flajole, SJ
Winfield Fountain
Louis Gaffney, SJ
Joseph Gardiner
Leila Gibbons
James Gilmore, SJ
James Goodwin, SJ
William Guppy
Margaret Haggerty
Helen Hanify
Vernon Harkins, SJ
Robert Harmon
Virginia Harmon
Patrick Hayes
Eugene Healy, SJ
Hildegard Hendrickson
Marvin Herard
Helon Hewitt
Jimmy Higashi
Lee Hodson
Jeanette Hulburt
Dolly Ito
Dolores Johnson
Warren Johnson
Francis Kane, SJ
George Keough
Harry Kinerk
James King, SJ
George Kunz
Charles LaCugna
Val Laigo
Robert Larson
Mary Alice Lee
Albert Lemieux, SJ
Marie Leonard
William LeRoux, SJ
Francis Lindekugel, SJ
Francis Logan, SJ
Reba Lucey
Paul Luger, SJ
Kenneth MacLean

Harry Majors Jr.
Donald Malins
Albert Mann
Maxime Marinoni
Clair Marshall, SJ
Eunice Martin
Ann Matuszewski
David McCloskey
Francis McGarrigle, SJ
James McGoldrick, SJ
James McGuigan, SJ
Thomas McInerney
William McLelland
Roberta McMahon, OP
Agnes McNulty
Edmund McNulty, SJ
Jean Merlino
Paul Milan
Joseph Monda
Jeanette Murphy
Raymond Nichols, SJ
Edward O'Brien
Ralph O'Brien
Thomas O'Brien, SJ
Cornelius O'Leary, SJ
Sally Olson
Thomas Page
James Parry
Mary Pearce
Blanche Perusse
Jane Peterson
Ronald Peterson
Mary Pirrung
Vincent Podbielancik
Christopher Querin, SP
David Read
Robert Rebhahn, SJ
James Reichmann, SJ
Daniel Reidy, SJ
Mary Ridge
Ben Robel

Stephen Robel
Theodore Ross
James Royce, SJ
Robert Saltvig
George Santisteban
Louis Sauvain, SJ
Leo Schmid, SJ
David Schroeder
Richard Schwaegler
John Schwarz, SJ
Francis Smedley
Robert Smith
Eunice Spencer
Edward H. Spiers
Bernard Steckler
Harriet Stephenson
John Talevich
William Taylor
Michael Taylor, SJ
David Tinius
Burnett Toskey
Michael Toulouse, SJ
John Toutonghi
Rosaleen Trainor, CSJ
Kathleen Treseler
Alan Troy
Richard Turner Jr.
Usha Varanasi
Robert Viggers
Paul Volpe
Kathleen Waters
Genevieve Weston
Charles Wollesen, SJ
Francis Wood, SJ
Dolly Wright
Marylou Wyse
Charles Yackulic
Andre Yandl
Barbara Yates
Anita Yourglich
Gary Zimmerman

THE SEATTLE UNIVERSITY JESUIT COMMUNITY IN 1991

Pictured from left to right, Jesuit Fathers John Topel, James Reichmann, Mark Goehring, Pat Howell, John Schwarz, Robert Grimm (Rector), Gregg Wood, Gerald Cobb (center rear), William LeRoux (center front), Emmett Carroll, Richard Ahler, Michael Kelliher, Roger Gillis, John Foster, Robert Egan, Joseph Maguire, Richard Sherburne, and David Leigh. (Photo by Brad Reynolds, SJ).

Other members of the Seattle University Jesuit Community and Loyola Hall residents in 1991 not pictured:
Jesuit Fathers William Bischoff, Francis Bisciglia, Roger Blanchette, Hugh Boyle, Robert Flack, Ronald Funke, Louis Gaffney,
Thomas Garvin, James Goodwin, James Harbaugh, Albert Haven, William Joyce, John Kelley, Patrick Kenny,
Henry Kohls, Francis Logan, Phil Lucid, John McCluskey, Alexander McDonald, Joseph McGowan, James McGuigan,
George McMonagle, Arthur McNeil, Gerard Morin, Jack Murphy, Francis Nawn, Joseph O'Connell, Cornelius O'Leary, Thomas O'Shea,
Lammert Otten, Robert Rebhahn, Robert Rekofke, James Royce, Louis Sauvain, James Selinsky, Thomas Sexton, Terrence Shea,
Robert Spitzer, William Sullivan, Raymond Talbott, Michael Taylor, Guy Ward, Frank Wood, James Wood, and Theodore Zombal.
(Special thanks to Laura Belcher, Minister's Assistant and Loyola Hall Secretary/Receptionist for the roster above.)

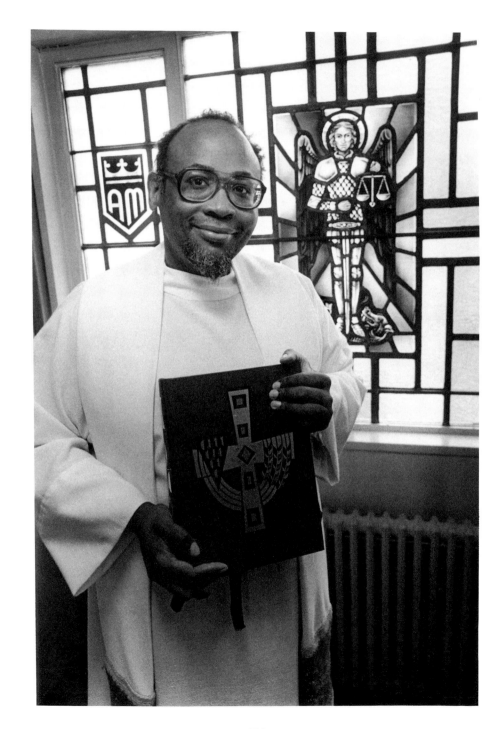

*Fr. Joseph O. McGowan,
SJ, directed the office for
minority affairs in the
1970s, the campus min-
istry in the 1980s, and
now coordinates the
Center for Peace and Jus-
tice. (Brad Reynolds, SJ)*

120

Fr. James Royce, SJ, became one of the world's leading experts on alcoholism as a byproduct of trying to counsel students with drinking problems. (Brad Reynolds, SJ)

Fr. Frank Wood, SJ, parlayed a life-long fascination with computers into one of the world's first curricula devoted to software engineering. (Brad Reynolds, SJ)

Fr. Louis Sauvain, SJ, and Fr. Joseph Maguire, SJ, seated in the Administration Building's original chapel, have provided counsel and support to generations of students and alumni. (Brad Reynolds, SJ)

Fr. William LeRoux, SJ, guided the School of Arts and Sciences through one of its roughest passages and helped to plan the revolutionary Matteo Ricci College. (Brad Reynolds, SJ)

Fr. Louis Gaffney, SJ, revived the university's spirit and finances in the early 1970s with his "contagious optimism" and creative academic reforms. (Brad Reynolds, SJ)

AUTHOR'S ACKNOWLEDGEMENTS

When I first met with Father Sullivan in July 1990 to begin work on this book, I asked if he wanted a real history or public relations puffery. "A history," he replied, and that is what we have endeavored to produce.

The narrative relies chiefly on the printed record, including minutes, correspondence, reports, and journalistic accounts. In the course of sifting through these materials, I developed a deep respect for the professionalism of the university's public information officers and its student journalists, who compiled a surprisingly fair and accurate record of the institution's life and activities. The work of John Talevich, Jean Merlino, Ed Donohoe, Fred Cordova, Bill Sears, Jack Gordon, and generations of *Spectator* reporters and editors made my task much easier.

These materials were preserved over the decades thanks to the diligence of university archivist Father Alexander McDonald, SJ, and his predecessor, the late Father Vincent Conway, SJ. Scores of individuals supplemented the printed record with their personal recollections and offered a sense of the quality of university life during various periods.

Such research was aided immeasurably by the far better historians who preceded me. This book could not have been produced in the time available (if at all) had not Father Tim Cronin, SJ, so expertly chronicled Seattle University's first 75 years and the parallel development of Catholic pedagogy in his 1982 doctoral thesis. Additionally, Father Wilfred Schoenberg, SJ, provided numerous details and insights in his comprehensive and delightful histories of the Catholic Church and Jesuit experiences in the Pacific Northwest. Finally, I found myself turning, as always, to Murray Morgan's *Skid Road* for the flavor of Seattle's past. I am very grateful that these three distinguished scholars took the time

to review the manuscript for this history and to offer valuable suggestions for its refinement.

The historical illustrations for this book derive chiefly from the university's archives, but some of the most important images were secured through the aid of Father Neill Meany, SJ, head of the Oregon Provincial Archives at Gonzaga University; Sister Rita Bergamini, director of the Sisters of Providence Archives in Seattle; and Paul Dorpat, Seattle's all-but-official visual archivist. I owe special thanks to the SU alumni who raided their family albums for unique photographs.

Father Brad Reynolds, SJ, created the vivid portraits of today's Jesuits and Chris Nordfors, Seattle University's staff photographer, captured the color panorama of the modern campus and much of the visual record of recent events. That these images combine with historical photos and the text to create a coherent and attractive whole is entirely the achievement of Marie McCaffrey, the designer of this book (and, incidentally, my wife), aided by the skilled graphic arts and printing professionals who participated in preparing this book.

Ultimate credit for this book belongs above all to the remarkable members of the Centennial Book Committee (listed at the beginning of the book) who suffered the cruel and unusual punishment of reading and rereading outlines, sketches, drafts and galleys over the past year and whose sage counsel lifted this project over many obstacles. While each made an important contribution, I want to make special mention of the aid and support provided by Zia Gipson, who coordinated the entire centennial observance, and Valerie Ryan, who had a great notion that the university needed a book like this and served as my chief editorial advisor. Thanks are also owed to the many members of the university staff who cheerfully responded to my often desperate cries for help; the tolerant staff at Gogerty & Stark who printed thousands of manuscript pages; and to Joe Devine, who cast his professional grammarian's eye over the manuscript and galleys. One other individual deserves to be singled out for his mentorship and guidance, but he will remain unnamed here at his request.

Finally, I must acknowledge the contributions of Father Sullivan. This volume would not exist without his support, and his rigorous skepticism made this a much better book than it might otherwise have been.

This is not to say that alumni and veterans of the staff and faculty may not find cause to quibble with things said or not said in these pages. As with all history, this book is an interpretation of other people's experiences, thoughts and actions. Any chronicler must make judgments in selection, emphasis and analysis, and they will never satisfy everyone. Whatever my errors of omission or commission, readers should find the overall portrait to be a faithful representation of its subject.

In closing, I want to say how much I have come to admire Seattle University and the people who built and sustained it in the face of challenges that would have daunted Job. Since I am neither a Catholic nor an alumnus and had never dealt with the institution prior to this commission, Seattle University was truly a discovery for me, and, yes, a revelation.

Publication of this book brings the year of my own "Jesuit education" to a close. If these pages have inspired a better appreciation of Seattle University and its mission, then our efforts will have earned a passing grade.

Walt Crowley
July 1991

Seattle University Campus

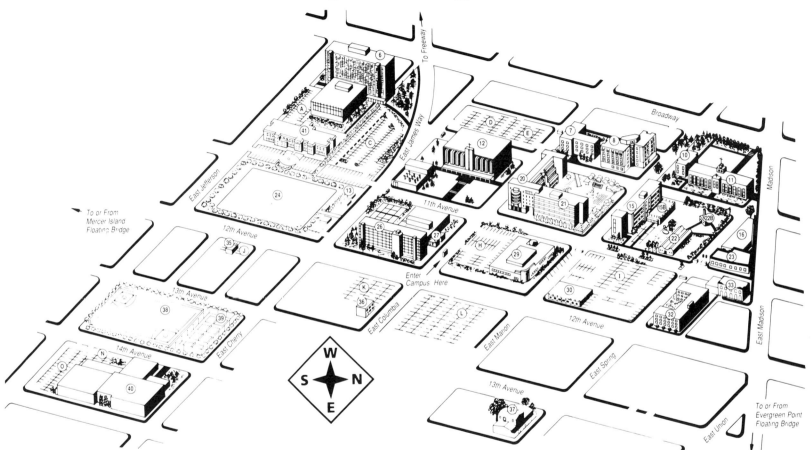

Legend

Note: Building numbers on map correspond to signs in front of buildings.

  Accessible entrance and elevator
  Accessible entrance to one floor
  Not accessible
DP Disabled parking

Campus Buildings

Administration Building 11
Bannan Building 21
Bellarmine Residence Hall 26
Bessie Burton Sullivan
Care Center 41
Buhr Hall 22
Campion Tower 6
Campus Services Building 30
Casey Building 8
Child Care Center 37
Connolly Center 40
Connolly Center Parking ....N DP

Engineering Building 20
Faculty/Staff Parking ...A, E, G, I, J, N
Fourteenth Ave. Sports Field 38
Garrand Building 10
International Student Center 13
Intramural Field 24
Lemieux Library 12
Loyola Hall 7
Lynn Nursing Building 33
Madison Building 16
McGoldrick Student Center 27
Pigott Building 15

Pigott Auditorium 15B
Sculpture Lab 22B
Seaport Building 36
Student Parking ....B, CDP, D. K,
....L DPN
Student Union 23
Tennis Center 39
Twelfth Avenue Building 35
University Services Building 29
Visitor Parking ....DP H
Xavier Residence Hall 32

127